The

AWAKENED

GUIDE

The
AWAKENED
GUIDE

THE NEXT WAVE

A Manual for Leaders, Teachers, Coaches, Healers, and Helpers

ELI JAXON-BEAR

The Awakened Guide

2020 by Eli Jaxon-Bear

New Morning Books Ashland, OR U.S.A. (541) 201-0900
www.newmorningbooks.com

Interior Design and Cover Design by Alan Dino Hebel
and Ian Koviak (theBookDesigners)

ISBN: 978-1-7329523-7-9

Dedicated to Gangaji, my life-long partner and best friend.
Without her clarity and depth of character none of this would be possible.

Also thank you to all who helped make this work possible. For the editorial help of Leigh Estok, Jared Franks, Clivia von Dewitz, Margi Wainio, as well as the many editors and users of this manual over the past twenty years, I am deeply grateful. And to the staff and students of The Leela School who have used, modified and brought this manual to life I send my love and gratitude.

FOREWORD

by Dr. Murray Korngold

In the West, those who are troubled by inner torment or are searching for fulfillment have long been conditioned and burdened, in their search for relief, by psychological concepts dating from Freud, Jung, and Adler. I find Eli Jaxon-Bear's work particularly relevant because I was personally involved in the psychological revolution starting in the late nineteen forties after World War II, when the psychology departments of colleges from coast to coast were flooded by returning GIs, like myself, who mostly rejected drive-directed or habit-directed personality theories in search of a deeper humanism.

While speaking the language of Freud, we were largely drawn and excited by what we thought of at that time as the third force, a new approach. In their pioneering work, the non-directivists became the "True Friends" of their therapy clients. This is the first clinical use of this relationship, which Eli develops into a high art. For *The Awakened Guide*, Eli Jaxon-Bear is uniquely qualified to teach strategy and tactics for clearing the decks to facilitate direct contact with spirit. Jaxon-Bear uses therapeutic trance work to help his students wake up from their personal trances of suffering in order to realize their true natures.

Possibly the best kept secret in modern times and certainly in the Western world is the fact that most humans spend almost all their waking lives beyond early childhood in a state of trance. It is a trance that equates language with reality and imagines a personal "I" in charge of life. Paradoxically this trance is the ultimate stance for survival, while guaranteeing we miss the essential qualities of what makes life worth living.

I am truly amazed at the way that the spiraling history of the craft of counseling and psychotherapy has evolved in presenting the teacher and guide as the True Friend. In the use of trance to achieve this goal, Jaxon-Bear is transforming clinical therapeutic practice by bypassing the endless stories of the egoic mind.

In this handbook for teachers and therapists, it is possible to directly experience the premise that Eli proposes: the mystic vision is purely and simply the acceptance of reality without any filters or maps. By mapping the client's reality and then altering it, Jaxon-Bear shows us how to then take away the map and reveal reality. This is a revolutionary use of therapeutic techniques. We can at last transcend the ego, the holy grail of therapy since Jung.

Jaxon-Bear's training and life history span the mystics of the three monotheisms, as well as their Buddhist and Hindu counterparts. His experience infuses his teaching with a deep spiritual flavor. From trance-dancing with Sufis in Morocco, to practicing visualizations with Tibetan Buddhists in California, to dharma combat in a Zen Monastery in Japan, he has directly experienced the variety of paths to the truth. But it is his ability to bring his revolutionary political sensibility to bear on ending suffering in the world that marries the material with the eternal. It is from this platform that his proposal of universal self-realization is to be reckoned with.

In the end, the author discovered lasting fulfillment, which required him to transcend all barriers to realization. As an experienced Zen practitioner and a student of Western psychology, he learned very early on that the realization of freedom and peace could only be achieved by bypassing the personal identity, acquired not only genetically but also by cultural conditioning (traditionally referred to as the ego).

Meister Eckhart, a true mystic of the fourteenth century was the first churchman to preach to his parishioners in the people's language, German, instead of the traditional Latin. Anyone can read Eckhart's twenty-fourth sermon entitled, "Blessed Are the Poor," which concludes with the ego-transcending message: "I have nothing, I know nothing, I am nothing." This is the fruit of realization that Eli's work evokes.

The egoic identity finds this terrifying. Most therapies are aimed at producing clients who are empowered to be someone special (while fulfilling desires), and to be someone inflated, self-important, and confident that the world is there for the taking. We have found over the decades that this does not lead to true happiness or fulfillment. The great mystery is that by being no one, the overflowing love of the cosmos is revealed to be one's true self. Sufi mystics, Chassidic mystics, and a variety of Christian saints all tell us the same message.

There are no exclusion clauses in student admissions to Eli's study of the way of realization. Atheists, agnostics, Christians, Jews, Moslems, and even Vedantists—believers and non-believers alike—may now, with the help of a True Friend, attain true self-knowledge, freedom, and peace.

— Dr. Murray Korngold
San Francisco, CA, 2014

Dr. Murray Korngold is a Founder of Los Angeles Society of Clinical Psychologists, having studied with Bruno Klopfer, an associate of Karl Jung. (Klopfer developed the Rorschach protocol and brought it to the US). Murray also studied with Helmut Kaiser, Wilhelm Reich's associate, in Los Angeles from 1956-1958. He then shared a practice with R.D. Laing in Kingsley Hall from 1964 to 1969. An author and teacher, Korngold founded the L.A. Free Clinic, and served in private practice in psychotherapy in San Francisco until his death in 2017.

The NEXT WAVE

by Dr. Yigal Joseph

The fundamental teachings that fashion the core of *The Awakened Guide* are two-fold. Eli Jaxon-Bear has characterized them both as reflections of the sacred. The first points to the formless teaching that inheres in the silent transmission of the truth, begin with: "Being quiet long enough and listening deeply enough that you fall back into yourself … realizing the unchanging silence that's the core of your being."

The second is the teaching in the form of skillful means: "The ability to move through the trance of the world without being entranced, without being distracted, without being withdrawn, fully embodied in service, fully embodied in yourself as yourself."

Jaxon-Bear has described the sacred teachings in form as having come to us "over thousands of years" bringing in "all the spiritual roots" of Hinduism, Buddhism, and ancient Greece. As you delve deeply into *The Awakened Guide*, you recognize that the skillful means it highlights also parallel, but are not limited to, the constructs and strategies of a tapestry of psychologies, which have evolved since the inception of modern psychology around 1879 in the Leipzig research laboratories of Wilhelm Wundt, considered "the father of experimental psychology."

The European Age of Enlightenment brought with it a fascination with psychology as seen in the works of Leibnitz and Kant. While Wolff identified psychology as an empiric science, writing *Psychologia Empirica* in 1732, Kant emphasized the Latin derivative of the prefix "psyche," i.e., the animating spirit of soul.

The inauguration of Wundt's laboratory in Leipzig prior to the turn of the 20th century was a momentous occasion for stimulating the opening of psychology laboratories across Europe and in the United States. By 1910, the definition of psychology relied on English derivatives of psyche to mean mind rather than soul.

The experimentalists flourished at the inception of the 20th century and made certain to distinguish themselves from parapsychologists and hypnotists, who became ostracized after having reached the zenith of their popularity in the previous century. It is noteworthy that the presuppositions that buttress *The Awakened Guide* reconcile these schisms of superficial understanding by elucidating how our present reality is constructed.

Much as in Rumi's parable of the "Blind Men and the Elephant," varying approaches to studying the mind and its grasp of reality have evolved. As psychological research unfolded, it tackled the question of why we do what we do from different vantage points, including the biological, the behavioral, the cognitive, the psychodynamic, the humanistic, the evolutionary, and the cross-cultural; each perspective attempting to touch and define the elephant in the room; each offering a relative truth for understanding the mind; each approach favored by varying interests in our society, such as pharmaceutical and health insurance companies, academia, etc.

As you explore the depths and range of *The Awakened Guide*, you will discover that it honors some aspect of the skillful means proposed by these psychological perspectives without being a sole proponent of any one or the other. For example, you will read Jaxon-Bear's take on Freud and see that, despite criticism of the limitations of his approach, he regards some Freudian terms such as the unconscious, ego, superego, drives, and instincts as useful constructs when dexterously working with the challenges that individuals may face. In this vein, subsequent researchers of psychodynamic processes, such as separation and individuation, have described the relationship between mother and child as coming out of symbiosis. The strength of that relationship has been viewed as analogous to the sacred holding space of the therapeutic relationship, which is also emphasized in this manual.

The behavioral and cognitive approaches in psychology have touched on stimulus-response conditioning, as well as the Interplay of core beliefs, triggering events, thoughts, emotions and physiological sensations, which may lead to significant mental, emotional, and behavioral reactions. As you will see as you explore the skillful means emphasized in *The Awakened Guide*, these underlying cognitive-behavioral processes of mind are quite helpful in working with the issues we and others may face in navigating the world.

In keeping with that view, we can now appreciate the reliance on clinical hypnosis as a skillful means represented in *The Awakened Guide*. While hypnosis has been stigmatized in the general culture as simply a novel parlor trick, since the 1950s it has enjoyed support in the medical community as an effective adjunct for treating various disorders.

More recently, researchers at Stanford and Columbia Universities, as well as at the University of Oregon, have studied the cognitive-behavioral dynamics of hypnosis. They've noted that the direction of cognitive processing is usually bottom-up, i.e., a sensation engenders a perception, which then triggers a cognitive overlay that gives meaning to the perception. Yet, we can also experience a top-down process in which a higher cortical cognition or thought engenders perceptions and subsequent sensations, e.g., as observed in the placebo effect. These researchers, utilizing the biological, neuroscience approach of brain studies with subjects in a trance, have observed that top-down cognitive processing occurs during hypnosis, in which an activated thought can engender perceptions that induce physical sensations.

The skillful means of clinical hypnosis emphasized in *The Awakened Guide* transcends its use for the amelioration of symptomatology in order to address the fundamental roots of suffering. This view is highlighted by the presuppositions identified in the Guide, for example:

Everyone is living in a waking trance we call ego. We do not see the world as it is, but rather as our projection.

    A. This trance state involves the physical, emotional, and mental aspects of our brain giving our experience a sense of reality.

    B. Trance is consensual. The personal trance that "I am my name, my body, my thoughts, and feelings" is reinforced by the shared belief of those around us.

    C. All trance states require a narrative. The narrative gives meaning to objects and events that arise and creates a sense of causality, requiring a past and a future.

    D. Waking up from the personal trance leads to self-realization. A self-realized person is free of illusion and filled with a sense of fulfillment and can lead a happy productive life.

Putting to rest the controversies around hypnosis, we can look towards Jaxon-Bear's guidance regarding skillful means: "It's all about function, not ideas or beliefs. If it doesn't work, try something else. If it works, stay true."

Similarly, the use of Neuro-Linguistic Programming (NLP), as highlighted in *The Awakened Guide*, has recently been better understood by the research community when viewed through the lens of cognitive-behavioral approaches. Both share common roots and work to create descriptive models of behavior as sequences of thoughts, perceptions, emotional responses, and reactions.

In cognitive-behavioral disciplines, a compendium of thoughts, emotions, and behaviors can be organized as the general schemata underlying particular diagnostic conditions, such as depression or anxiety. NLP, however, looks at client-specific internal representations rather than generalized schemata of particular mental states. Researchers have recently observed that, when generalized cognitive-behavioral schemata are addressed within the NLP framework of individuality, behavioral changes can be more readily studied and observed. It is further postulated that when NLP client-specific internal representations are considered, the recidivism currently observed in cognitive-behavioral interventions may be diminished.

As you will discover when you sincerely investigate *The Awakened Guide*, it utilizes the skillful means of Clinical Hypnosis, Neuro-Linguistic Programming and Cognitive-Behavioral therapies on one of three levels: symptom removal, ego strengthening, and ego transcendence. In each case, the client's map of reality is significantly altered; neurotic patterns of ideation and feeling are untangled; and the possibility naturally arises that the identification of self can shift from the personal to the transcendental, i.e., from identification with "me and mine" to the timeless, spaceless, empty consciousness that is the root and substance of all manifestation.

And herein lies the unique power and elegance that is on display in *The Awakened Guide*. While it engages in the dialectics of psychological approaches that attempt to map the mind, it transcends them by not mistaking the maps for the territory; it is neither defined nor delimited by them. Recall that the primary sacred teachings elucidated by Jaxon-Bear were in the realm of the formless, which inheres in the silent transmission of the truth of yourself, and the teaching in form of skillful means. The two teachings seamlessly converge and are simultaneously contained in the profound stance of the True Friend, which serves as *The Awakened Guide's* model for negotiating the vagaries of the world, as well as the benchmark for all authentic interpersonal relationships including that of client and therapist.

Eli Jaxon-Bear has described this radical stance as follows: "Being a True Friend in our context is the ability to be with someone with an open heart and a silent mind in order to receive them without anything going on internally: no judgment, no desire to help or fix, not needing anything back, like love or recognition or support. In this way the person in need can be in a completely safe space and receive a true reflection of themselves in a moment of openness, silence, and love."

Dr. Joseph served as Chief Psychologist of the Corsello Centers for Complimentary Medicine; and as Director of the NYC Psychologist-In-Training Program, where he coordinated the recruitment, training, and supervision of psychology interns in collaboration with ten area colleges and universities. As senior administrator in the Office of Schools' Chancellor, he enabled school leadership teams to incorporate exemplary teaching and learning standards.

INTRODUCTION

by Eli Jaxon-Bear

My teacher gave me an assignment and a challenge: to bring the direct realization of what Zen calls "No-Mind" into the realm of therapy and spiritual healing. He said, "Let both client and therapist wake up." What he called No-Mind is the living transmission of silence that ends all misidentification. When mistaken identity stops, the direct realization of your true nature is possible beyond thought, concept, or doubt. Living with a silent mind and an open heart mark the end of therapy and are the ultimate healing for both therapist and client. This book is a map for ending false identification and a guidebook for skillful means.

The goal of a therapist is to be a True Friend in the deepest sense through your own direct realization. You cannot take anyone further down the spiritual path than you have traveled yourself. The great tendency is to preach or "talk about" which conceptualizes and makes false whatever truth may be spoken. Better to just be quiet with no need to share. Let the silent majesty within radiate and all will benefit without words.

A Silent Mind is the end of the spiritual search, the end of the journey, and the beginning of an awakened life. Then you naturally are a True Friend to yourself and the world, regardless of the role that may appear.

When you do not have a personal agenda for how the moment should be, you can experience the moment as an intimate embrace. You will be more efficient, and you will be more productive, because you will not be engaged in internal dialog about what you should or should not be doing. Once the commentator is gone, you can directly experience life. This is not disassociation and does not involve any practice or concept or memory. It cannot be forgotten or remembered.

This is both the end and the beginning. The old life is left in ashes and the new is just dawning.

You cannot force realization any more than you can build true character. What you can do is be willing for whatever it takes to realize the truth. This willingness will be confronted by fixation and its attendant habits of mind, emotions, and body. Willingness will pierce the veils and lead to realization.

In staying true to willingness in the face of fixation, true character emerges. Full realization with true character is the pinnacle of our possibility as humans.

This is the still point at the center of the universe. I call it Home.

—Eli Jaxon-Bear

Contents

FOUNDATION *of* LEELA THERAPY

PRESUPPOSITIONS

- Everyone is living in a waking trance we call ego. We do not see the world as it is, but rather our projection of it. The trance is based on the belief that: "I know who I am. I know what I am. I know where I am." All belief is a trance state.

- This trance state involves the physical, emotional, and mental aspects of our brain giving our experience a sense of reality. We believe what we sense, feel, and think to be real. We call this personal reality "I," "myself," and it is clinically called the egoic sense of self. It is marked by suffering.

- Trance is consensual. The personal trance that "I am my name, my body, my thoughts, and feelings" is reinforced by the shared belief of those around us, starting with our parents or earliest care givers. The personal trance is nested inside the family trance, nested inside the community and the tribal trance, nested inside the global trance. If, for example you stop believing that pieces of paper called money have value, the trance of money does not stop as long as everyone else still believes in it.

- All trance states require a narrative. The narrative gives meaning to objects and events that arise and creates a sense of causality, requiring a past and a future.

- Waking up from a consensual trance brings disillusionment. For example, to go from believing in a particular religion to seeing through it leads to a sense of liberation from the trance and the despair of being disillusioned. To be disillusioned is to wake up from the illusion of the trance. This leads to both a momentary sense of freedom and a sense of alienation or separation which is an essential stage in waking up from the personal trance. Waking from a particular consensual trance can be a prelude to waking up from the personal trance, as the first awakening leads to a sense of isolated separateness. Alienation is part of the individuation process that frees our attention enough so that it can be directed inwards.

- Waking up from the personal trance leads to self-realization. A self-realized person is free of illusion and filled with a sense of fulfillment and can lead a happy productive life without the constraints of self-doubt or a sense of un-lovability and despair that mark the ego state of personal trance. Waking up from the personal trance leads to what has been the elusive goal of lasting happiness based in fulfillment rather than external circumstances.

LEVELS OF THERAPY

All therapy happens within the parameters of the physical, mental and emotional realms. This is characterized by the triangle of behavior, thoughts, and feelings used in the CBT (Cognitive Behavioral Therapy) model.

Therapy happens on one of three levels: symptom removal, ego strengthening, ego transcendence.

- Symptom removal is characterized by a change in behaviors, thoughts and feelings. A variety of therapies address this level. We use the NLP model as a fast and effective way of changing behaviors, thoughts and feelings. NLP presents us with a wide variety of insights and interventions in the client's map of reality, leading to cascading changes.

- Ego strengthening involves working on the egoic sense of lack of self-worth. There is an inherent sense of lack present in all egoic states at some level. For most it is sublimated enough to have what Freud characterized as normal suffering, which he saw as inescapable. When the person is handicapped by their sense of egoic insufficiency, this unbalanced state will be centered in the emotional and mental realms leading to changes in behavior. Relaxation techniques and meditation practices of the third wave may address this level of healing by calming the mind and developing the discipline of a meditation practice, thus breaking the neurotic patterns of ideation and feeling.

- ○ Being a True Friend models the possibility for the client of being free of neurotic patterns. The simple act of sitting as a True Friend with a quiet mind and an open heart has a salubrious effect on the neurochemistry of the client.

- ○ Leela Therapy also addresses this realm through the skill of the True Friend in helping to elicit a diagnosis of both the presenting state and the desired state. This diagnosis and projected outcome address the thoughts, emotions and behaviors of the presenting problem and the outcome and follow the NLP model. The art of the True Friend and any exceptional therapy is the capacity to intervene at the critical junction point where insight into the egoic wounding can lead to emotional healing and a more fulfilling, less stressful life.

- Ego transcendence happens when the personally identified consciousness reflects on itself and is willing to turn away from everything that it considers real to find the illuminating consciousness that is shining from behind the realm of thoughts feeling and behaviors. When this conscious reflection of consciousness upon itself without an object is one-pointed and concentrated, the identity of self can shift from the personal to the transcendental. Instead of identifying oneself with the different forms of manifestation, one identifies as the timeless, spaceless, empty consciousness that is the root and substance of all manifestation.

This awakening to one's true nature reveals the answers to the questions of who am I? What am I? Where am I? Having only the cognitive information to these answers, even if correct, without the direct transcendent experience leads to a conceptualization that imitates true realization but does not bring the full benefit of direct knowing that is beyond knowing.

METHODS OF THERAPY

- Change the Map: Changing the Narrative. All meaning of self and other is derived from the narrative. By changing the narrative, the relatively experienced reality based on the personal map changes. The narrative is a blend of images, sounds, sensations, and vocalized thoughts.

○ NLP use of sub-modalities and reframing to change the map, which changes the narrative.

○ Hypnotic altered state stops the narrative and can alter the map

○ Self-reflection can change the map and the narrative by reflecting on what had been subconscious patterns.

- Altered States: Hypnosis. Just as environmentally-produced altered states such as shock or terror can produce long-lasting or permanent changes in the neurology of the brain as in the creation of PTSD, so can positive environmental agents like psychedelics cause deep and lasting positive change. I have found clinical hypnosis to be a safe and easily controlled method for producing an altered state and entering the deep symbolic layers of the psyche. MRI's have conclusively shown that decision making takes place below the conscious level, with the decision being made before the conscious mind thinks that it is making the decision. This is the level where lasting therapeutic change takes place and is easily accessed by the altered state of hypnosis.

- Limbic Bonding: True Friend. Simply by the ability of the therapist to enter rapport with the client changes in the client's physiology can occur as shown by the non-directive therapist. If the internal state of the therapist is what we are calling a True Friend, having a quiet mind, an open heart and being fully available to pacing the client's presenting reality, profound change can occur. When the True Friend also has the skillful means of inducing altered states through trance and the skills and insights of the leverage points of the narrative, deep and lasting changes can be affected in the client's presenting problem and sense of self.

- Ego transcendence arises from intense self-examination and the willingness to not fall back into the habitual movements of mind. When the structure and vocabulary of ego are clearly understood and recognized in what one calls "me," there is the possibility to not identify with the egoic impulses by experiencing whatever arises fully, and not move with the habitual patterns of ego. In not moving, the impulse is experienced as a fire, burning the old conditioned pattern. This burning opens the possibility of falling deeper into oneself, beyond the realm of thoughts, emotions and sensations to fall into the timeless, silent realm of true self.

Let Both Client *and* Therapist Wake Up

Through the 1980s I led the Clinical Hypnosis Certification Program at Esalen Institute, in Big Sur, California and at the Institut Dr. Schmida in Vienna, Austria. This month-long training was a synthesis of the Enneagram with Neurolinguistics and Ericksonian Hypnosis. At the time, I was certified as a Master Trainer in Neurolinguistics and was on the Board of Examiners of the American Council of Hypnotist Examiners. Many people who went through this program are now successful therapists, teachers and spiritual leaders.

After an eighteen-year spiritual search, when I met my final teacher, in January 1990, everything stopped. My teacher, Sri Poonjaji, asked me to return to the world of therapy so that "both client and therapist can wake up!"

This manual is the distilled essence of those past trainings held now in the context of silence and awakening. The skills of observant insight and skillful means are in service of silence. In this way, the role of therapist has evolved into the role of a True Friend. Put what you read here into practice and it is possible to be a True Friend for the world. Regardless of your life circumstances these skillful means will give you the possibility of true service in all your relationships.

As a helping professional in any capacity you will discover that the ground of being a True Friend will be the reservoir of skillful means and the source of inspired, insightful intervention. Being a therapist is both a skill and an art. A computer can teach the skills but the artful expression will only come from the depth of your being. Wedding skill and art is a life-long practice. Practice leads towards perfection.

PART ONE

Being A Therapist

The WORK

In this book, beyond learning all the skills necessary to be a great therapist, you will discover, clearly and precisely, how you create the trance of suffering that you call by your name.

We all want to discover what it is that makes this illusion of "me and my life" seem so real. This illusion of egoic identity is mysteriously created by the perception of the senses combined with the physical, emotional, mental, and circumstantial bodies of individual manifestation. This illusion is then believed to be reality. But this is not reality; it is a trance induction. When you can clearly see how you create your own trance of suffering you will have compassion and the start of skillful means for helping others escape from the prison of their mind.

By examining the structure of the emotional and mental bodies and the senses down to their smallest experiential components, we are going to discover what makes the trance of "me" so believable. When you see how you are perpetuating unnecessary suffering for yourself and others, you will have the possibility of ending it. Essentially, our purpose here is to recognize and deepen into the truth of Being. By allowing yourself to clearly see how the truth gets veiled, covered, denied and imitated–you will greatly support this awakening.

When you see how your own trance works and how to wake up from it, you will quite naturally be a support for others who want to wake up from the trance they are in. Rather than supporting their story of suffering by agreeing with it, fighting with it or withdrawing from it – you can enter rapport with their experience and be of support in the process of discovering what is really here and who one really is. In this way, you can play the role of a True Friend.

LEVELS OF WORK

Change

Change is the first level of successful therapy. By using the insights in this book you will discover that you can work on the trance induction of ego and support positive change. On the level of ego, you can experience more success, more confidence, more relaxation, and heal old traumas and emotional wounds. You can change habits and patterns. You can change the way you perceive people, events and circumstances. You can make this dream of being an individual person a relatively good dream. Working on this level can be very powerful and appropriate; sometimes it is just what is needed.

Transcendence

When what is wanted and called for is ego transcendence, it is no longer a matter of changing or improving anything, but of seeing through the appearance of the dream to the reality of ever-present Being. If you as the True Friend are awake and see clearly, you are naturally a support for others who are called to come out of their trance of suffering. Awakeness itself, the Presence that shines through a silent mind, is the most fundamental support for transcending egoic mind.

"Be still," were the words of Ramana Maharishi. "Simply keep quiet, and make no effort," said Papaji. These words carry the transmission of silence and point to ever-present truth, which is revealed when the veils of thinking and doing are stilled. This teaching transmission points to the end of all efforts to improve, remedy, or change one's self or one's experience as a way to realize lasting peace, happiness and love. For those who are spiritually mature, and ready to give everything for the truth, the being of a true Teacher can penetrate beyond the mind and awaken the soul to its true nature.

The Approach

Fortunately, for souls who are called to end egoic suffering, but are seemingly not yet ripe enough to simply hear the truth spoken and turn away from the illusion, there is an approach. This approach is not about changing the appearance of egoic mind or of experience, but of recognizing it clearly and without judgment, and bearing the discomfort of this exposure. True self-inquiry is an unsentimental investigation of who and what you have identified yourself to be, in ever more subtle ways. The exposure of false identification in the context of a strong determination to reveal what is true burns up patterns of egoic illusion and opens the mind to the truth.

This insight is also a deep support after awakening: As latent tendencies arise, if they are clearly recognized they can be allowed to burn in the fire of direct experience. A direct and detailed understanding of how the veils of illusion are created will also be a great support for working with others on all levels. With this insight and your own realization, you can be a True Friend to others who are mistaking the illusion for reality, and who want to wake up from that illusion.

The Challenge and Work

In this process you are going to find that since you already are a master hypnotist and your own best subject, and since most everyone you meet is already in trance, using methods of hypnosis to lead others into trance is going to be the easiest part of what we are going to discover together. The real challenge is to wake up from the trance you are already in, and to not go back to sleep.

INTRODUCTION *to* ETHICS

SACRED SPACE

Sacred Space is how we refer to confidentiality in this work, as well as in the Client-Therapist relationship. The space within which anything can be revealed without the stress and worry that what is said may end up being revealed outside of the therapy room. It is an obligation of the True Friend and Therapist to keep what is said private and confidential, but also to not use what is said in a later conversation outside of the therapy room. If you meet your client in the street, you do not refer to anything that has been said in Sacred Space. In fact, holding on to a story told by a client means the therapist is now in their own trance of suffering. The therapist lets the client or group know that the space is Sacred Space and this is a fundamental understanding of both the client and therapist.

RAPPORT

Rapport means that the therapist meets what is here. Whatever and however the client shows up in therapy is the starting point, and the True Friend can meet the client exactly where they are. This means there is a confirmation of what is showing up. It can involve the therapist saying "Yes" to whatever the client says, no matter what it is. It can also involve repeating back the words of the client. For example, the client may say "I am feeling so angry about what he just said to me!" to which the therapist replies, "Yes, you are feeling so angry about what he just said to you!" If this is spoken in a truly empathetic state it will be received. If it is done in an insincere way it will be rejected. In this way, you discover rapport with the client in order to better pace them and lead them to the desired state. Rapport can also mean mirroring physical gestures such as arms crossed or legs crossed, breathing rate, voice tone etc. Without rapport, it is very difficult to take the client deeper and can create tension and distrust. We will look more deeply into rapport later.

BOUNDARIES

Boundaries are important in all social relationships, including the client-therapist relationship. There are legally prescribed boundaries such as not having a sexual relationship with a client. There are also boundaries such as not having a friend or relative as a client due to confusion that can arise from having a historical relationship with the client. Clients can sometimes seek to contact the therapist outside of the client-therapist relationship with text messages or phone calls, which may not be appropriate. It is important that the therapist is upfront and clear about boundaries when something is happening that is not serving the client's or the therapist's best interests.

PROJECTION

Projection is the trance of associating your present emotions and thoughts with someone outside and telling a story about how they are responsible for them. This is a common mental process and can influence the client-therapist relationship in many ways. Clients can associate their new-found happiness or bliss that has resulted from the session with the therapist and form emotional bonds with the therapist based on this projection. This can include sexual attraction, projecting the father/mother, son/daughter relationship onto the therapist, and many more. It is important that the therapist is aware of these tendencies so as not to play into them or encourage them.

The POWER *of* THERAPEUTIC TRANCE

FREUD

At the beginning of his career, Sigmund Freud worked with Joseph Breuer's method of therapy for curing hysterics with the use of hypnosis. Breuer and then Freud were quite successful in treating hysteria, and Freud co-authored a paper with Breuer on their success. Unfortunately, however, Freud was perhaps not very adept at hypnosis, because he found that many of his patients, particularly non-hysterics, could not experience the hypnotic state. Consequently, he abandoned hypnosis and tried other methods to achieve that same broadness of mind and natural healing that often occurred in hypnosis.

His approach was to sit behind his client and work with dreams and associations to try and find a key to the subconscious, which had previously been revealed through hypnosis. Once Freudian analysis and later Jungian analysis became dominant in the newly emerging field of psychotherapy, hypnosis dropped away. Soon only performers were using hypnosis for stage shows. Hypnosis lost its legitimacy and status to talk-therapy. No self-respecting college graduate of my generation would be proud to go home to tell the parents that instead of entering the field of psychotherapy he or she had become a hypnotist. It would be a shame, a black mark, and a standing joke in the family, regardless of how effectively it worked in therapy. Even though it has always worked, hypnosis has had no real status or respect in the therapeutic community until recently.

Now it works at least as well as it did for Freud when he started out curing hysterics, and in fact magnitudes better, with many hospitals adopting it as part of their healing function.

Over the generations of post-Freudian insight, hypnotherapy has evolved beyond exploring the contents of the subconscious to actually mapping out its structure. Freud's insights were unfortunately well-mixed with his projections of his own mental structure, clouding the usefulness of this emerging model. We now better understand the wounding and healing of trauma and how the emotions are nested and layered, providing us with the way out of the nightmare trance of suffering.

A NEW MODEL OF MIND

As consciousness pioneers rediscover the power of an altered mind in service of reflection, hypnosis will again emerge as one of the most powerful and safe medicines for the damaged mind, as well as a means of transcendence and insight for the healthy mind. A damaged brain may require biochemical intervention, but a damaged ego can return to wholeness and then transcendence.

Freud imagined that the patient's failure to go into trance was what made hypnosis ineffective, when all along the problem lay in the therapist's lack of flexibility and skill. We now know that the patient is already in a deep trance. It is the skillful means of the True Friend to meet the trance of the client and stay in rapport.

If Freud had met Milton Erickson, we would be in a profoundly different mind space as a culture today. Dr. Erickson widened the possibilities of facilitating trance without a particular defined procedure. Milton Erickson was the master of showing us how even the most difficult of clients can be met and led into a deeply altered state.

HYPNOSIS AND INSIGHT

In my work with hypnosis, I found that it was possible for the client to enter a profound inner space, with an open mind, and to discover for him or herself what was real. This use of hypnosis in the service of insight is really what Freud was successfully using in his early career with Breuer's technique. Unfortunately, however, Freud stopped with the fact of egoic suffering and claimed that true happiness was not possible; we just needed to learn to live with our suffering in a non-neurotic way. Easier said than done, even in this very limited goal. The repeated failure to achieve this goal of non-neurotic suffering is because the nature of ego is both the cause of the suffering and the neurosis. The foxes are guarding the henhouse. This is why analysis can go on for years with few verifiable results.

As I began to work with people, I could see that hypnosis could be used to wake up from the trance of suffering, at least for a moment, and to learn how the trance was being constructed, followed, and believed. We can discover what happens when the trance called "my reality" disappears.

What *is* Therapeutic Trance?

Trance is an altered mind state that shuts down the cognitive thinking of the analytical part of one's mind. With trance it is possible to gain access to the wider, spacious aspect of the mind. Since the therapeutic trance state is occurring within the larger trance of the client's life, which is being called "reality," there has to be an even larger framework within which the trance state operates.

Trance work is usually used to work on habits and issues of self-esteem and the level of symptom removal and ego-strengthening. These are valuable and useful applications for the trance state, but the possibility is much greater depending on the depth of realization of the guide.

It is possible to enter the deep regions of the subconscious to address latent forms of egoic identification with suffering. Rather than working directly on the personality, but by working in the deeper regions, the personality will naturally change to reflect the deeper realizations. The key to this, however, is not how deep the client can go but how deep the guide is.

DEPTH

The great problem inherent in all forms of talk therapy is that it is a mental process. Rather than shutting it down, talking stimulates the thinking mind, even when talking about dreams. Consequently, any insights gained can be just as easily lost in the next conversation, unless these insights have been grounded into a level of being that is deeper than the conscious mind. This is why Cognitive Behavioral Therapy does not last. The insights are largely on the superficial personality level.

Most talk therapies usually assign causality in the wrong direction. Freud, in a very general sense, assigned causality of symptoms to a set of unresolved issues in the subconscious. Post-Freudians may also point to environmental causes of neurotic symptoms, and both of these approaches are correct to a degree, but what is missed is the structure of ego itself. At the root of all of it is the belief in the reality of a "me." For Freud, and for most therapists who came afterwards, the assumption has been that the ego is real. Subsequently most forms of psychotherapy actually strengthen the belief in the story of a "me," which is why Freud saw no way out and believed it impossible to have a happy fulfilled life.

Emotional Healing *and* *The* Limbic Brain

All mammals have a limbic brain; it is our emotional center. Mammals have emotions so that they can become bonded with their young and their support group. In nursing, a mother is giving her own stores of energy, her own life-force, to her offspring. She is not merely bringing them food like birds do, but they are feeding directly on her body. Emotional bonding allows this to happen without the babies being eaten as they are in species without an emotional brain.

Beyond raising our kin, the emotional brain allows us to survive by emotionally bonding with our group, from family to clan, kinship, tribe and nation. As mammals we could not survive without an emotional brain to keep us from killing each other even more than we already do.

Childhood wounding and other traumas are limbically generated and stored in what we are calling the emotional brain. We now know that memories are not discreet objects but are many different sensory signals stored in different parts of the brain. We have to tell ourselves a story in order to sequence these sensations into the apparent continuity that we call our life story. The emotional *me* is the feeling core of the egoic experience.

As we shall see the, ego is rooted in despair. And despair is both a no-exit situation and the gateway to liberation.

HEALING EMOTIONAL TRAUMA

With hypnosis, healing emotional trauma can happen rather quickly and easily in most cases.

This is at least partially because all memories are made up. We have to reconstruct them every time we remember them and each time, we change them. We do not remember the same detail and texture in each retelling because each time we remember we are laying down a new track. The limbic brain does not make a distinction between what really happened and what we remember happened. So we can change our memories by remembering them with a different emotional tone and different outcome.

POTENTIAL BENEFIT OF EMOTIONAL WOUNDING

But we must bear in mind that not all emotional wounding is negative or harmful. Egoic wounding is essential as part of the process of waking up. Just as a baby chick pecks from inside the shell, emotional wounding pierces the egoic shell from the outside allowing for egoic ideations to be seen through as non-existent. I have always distinctly remembered a moment of deep trauma at the age of three. This moment changed the direction of my life. It revealed a momentary glimpse behind the curtain of reality and put me on my life's course. I am forever grateful for this wounding. I would not be writing these words without it. It never needed healing.

HEALING EMOTIONAL WOUNDS

In healing childhood wounds there can be an assumption that they are real. This is a good assumption to make in the face of someone suffering from childhood wounds and the alliance of your agreement with their pain can help in the healing process. But if the helper believes the story, the helper often will become sentimentally attached to their own inner story and miss the essential. The art of therapy is noticing the essential and working with it structurally as we will see further on in this book. Healing emotional wounding can be a great liberation of energy or it can be a trap by making the belief in the story more concrete. This depends on the depth of the helper.

Trance work is the best way of working with the limbic brain. The limbic brain, which was our major hardware upgrade over the reptilian brain and has been around for millennia, doesn't make a distinction between what truly happened and what we imagine happened. It all depends on intensity and repetition.

We can go back to the memories of the wounding and change the experience to something useful.

The beautiful thing about Trance is that it turns off conversations, turns off the rumination center, the internal dialogue, the logical reasoning, so that you can drop into a direct experience, deeper than the conscious mind. Trance takes you out of your analytical mind and into the deeper spacious mind. It's a very useful altered state where the conscious mind is in a mysterious way bypassed and where healing takes place. Healing is the resolution of the story into a useful outcome. In large part this resolution comes from the realization that we each have all that we need.

A Model *for* Inquiry

Successful inquiry and therapeutic communication move from a Present Condition to a Desired Condition.

The Present Condition is what your friend or client comes to you with. It includes the mental, emotional, and physical state that they are presently experiencing–as well as their present realization of who they really are (Awareness, Emptiness, Love), which transcends and includes all states.

The Desired Condition is what they want to experience or realize. They may want to experience a more positive or resourceful state (mentally, emotionally, physically) in a particular context. Or, they may simply want to realize who they really are (Awareness, Emptiness, Love) regardless of what states may be present or not.

There are three levels of work:

The Symptom Level is where one may focus on undesirable emotional and behavioral responses such as phobias, smoking, overeating, nail biting etc. This is the most surface level.

Ego Strengthening works on a deeper level where the focus may be helping someone to discover more confidence, more self-esteem, more forgiveness, and self-acceptance.

Ego Transcendence is the deepest level. This is where one is ready to end the story of personal suffering and live in peace as the truth of who they are. This level points to the direct realization of non-dual reality, and the recognition and burning of the character fixation.

Ideally, as much as possible of the totality of the person is addressed, from the smallest part through all the bodies of manifestation into Essence and Self-Realization.

The ROLE *of* A THERAPIST

"There is no such thing as a resistant client, only an inflexible therapist." (Bandler and Grinder)

Good therapy happens when you discover that you are wisdom itself and that you have all the resources you need. Then naturally you will reflect this understanding to your client. You will see that the client is also wisdom itself and already has all the resources that they need.

What we are calling the client, is wisdom itself incarnate.

Wisdom itself incarnate needs nothing.

Your job as a therapist is merely to allow the client to uncover the veiling of ignorance to discover the truth. And then you will find that miracles happen.

TRAPS AND BELIEFS

One of the great traps of therapy is the belief that the therapist is going to give you something. If the therapist gives you something, even if it is wonderful, the presupposition of the relationship is that you are needy, and there is somebody else out there who has it, and that you have to go somewhere to get it. This might be useful at a stage of ego strengthening but ultimately must be seen through to the deeper wisdom alive in each heart. Everything needed is already present in your own heart. You just need to be quiet enough to listen, and willing enough to bear whatever might arise without moving.

Another great danger is that people searching for help are often filled with new beliefs as a means to overcome their difficulties. Whether it is a belief in Jesus or Buddha, or angels or prosperity consciousness or Cognitive Behavioral Therapy, a new ideology tends to replace one that is not working. New Gods replace the old Gods. The great tendency of mind is to create another structure and belief system to support the egoic identity.

We can be given new strategies to overcome fears, or learn how to have more success, to manifest wealth, how to be more popular, to get more, but this is another superficial form of attempted black magic. Luckily it does not ultimately work. Even if successful, it is not fulfilling. This can aid the ripening of the desire for truth and freedom.

WISDOM

Let it be as it is.
Untouched.
Untouched is not separate.

Be fully incarnate.
Be fully alive.
Fully present and untouched.

When we don't touch, don't interfere, don't interject our desires and opinions and attempts to control things, things take care of themselves. All knots unwind very naturally. Quite naturally we become more serene, more peaceful in our outlook, in our personality, in our lifestyle. That happens without doing anything as our natural bliss bubbles into life.

RULES

While there are many successful techniques in this book, our focus is not just about learning techniques. There are no rules. You won't have any rules or particular behavior patterns; like "every time this happens, I do that." Because if you do, you will be like just another robot; just like a rat running through a better maze. Instead you will discover spontaneous living beyond doubt. Most therapy is about techniques and diagnosis. Not that the techniques aren't useful, they give you a basis for skillful means, but there are no rules for which technique to use when, and, as a True Friend you will discover your own intuitive spontaneous response to what arises from the client.

EGO STRENGTHENING

As you sink more deeply into the truth of yourself, you will discover that sometimes when someone is suffering, it can be like being with a young child having a bad dream. Now, do you go over and shake the child awake?

No, you comfort the baby. I have been with children who are having nightmares, and while they are in their dreams, I have gone in and helped them with their nightmares, helped them to find resources within the dreams themselves to help with what's going on. If the bogeyman's chasing them, suddenly they can discover enormous courage, and they can have friends who help them in the dream. And they get through the nightmare. This is ego-strengthening.

You could say, "It's just a dream, it's not real." And at times that is appropriate. But usually it is spiritual preaching and we have all had enough preaching in this life. Often it is appropriate to enter the nightmare with them and show them that this is a chance to test their own courage and resourcefulness.

SKILLFUL MEANS

Two ways that as helpers we tend to fall off the edge: we get sentimentally attached to the story or we resist it in some way. The question is what really works? When you see someone suffering you don't want them to suffer. What is the most effective way to end suffering?

Allow spontaneity to come from silent wisdom informed by skillful means. Out of emptiness arises spontaneity. It might appear cold or it might appear hot. It might appear completely engaged, or it might appear completely disengaged. You cannot judge by the particular behavior, only the results.

The basic ground of being for any therapeutic work is to first be a True Friend to yourself! Allow whatever appears without judgment or blame. "Yes" is welcome, "No" is welcome. There may be a tendency to make "No" wrong, as if being open means you must say "yes," even when in your heart you know better.

It is not about right or wrong. You are free to be who you are, to experience both poles and all dualities. Skillful means come from not having any rules, yet are informed by insight and the tools of successful intervention.

Very often in therapy, the therapist is involved in the story and gives the client advice about how to change the story. The therapist is the one who has the answers, who has the power and insight about how to do it better. This book is not teaching that way. In fact, it is exactly the opposite. The only thing the therapist does is give the client permission to discover the wisdom already inside.

Your job as a True Friend is to serve as the space for the other to discover that they have all the resources they need. They can do their own work. Everyone is already inherent wisdom. Innate wisdom lives in the heart of every being. It doesn't need anything except unveiling from the cloud of personal identity.

PART TWO

Skills of A Therapist

The Structure of a Session

1. *True Friend*

2. *Rapport*

3. *Present Condition*

4. *Desired Condition*

5. *Anchoring*

6. *Induction*

7. *Intervention*

1. Being a True Friend

The basic foundation of this work is the position of what I call a "True Friend." A True Friend is solid and unmoving. A True Friend is open and fluid. A True Friend is deep and subtle. This stance supports everything else.

A True Friend holds no position for or against, does not agree or disagree. A True Friend is not full of answers and is not ignorant. In having no position, a True Friend can be an ally and a truth teller.

A True Friend is the open space where the light of consciousness can be reflected back upon itself.

To be open space is not to hold space, as there is no one holding anything. To be open space is the greatest gift that we can give one another. No training is needed, no qualification or practice, merely the willingness to be a silent loving being with no agenda. To be a True Friend is simply to be quiet and see.

When first faced with giving up our opinion or voicing our view, it may seem like a great sacrifice, the sacrifice of projecting and defending a personal trance that our minds typically call "reality." The willingness to stop and not follow the next impulse or thought reveals the silent awareness of being. This is what we all long for from ourselves and from each other.

The surest way to be a True Friend is this: First realize for yourself that there is a timeless, spaceless, formless, silent reality within you. This is the first step. It is a glimpse. It is not the end of the tunnel but the light that is at the end of the tunnel.

To catch a glimpse even for an instant behind the curtain of Maya (the illusory world) is enough to know for certain that nothing is as it appears. This is the crack in the cosmic egg that you can peck your way through simply with your willingness. The realization of silence within is the first step.

The next step is to surrender into that unknown empty space. Then your job is done. With nothing left to do, there is no need for movement or judgment or commentary. The mind can be completely still as it has no work to do. There is nothing to think about, to wonder about, to question. Just be still and see.

Next, realize yourself as the silent ground of being from which all phenomena arise. All transitory passing phenomena of all four bodies—mental, emotional, physical, and situational—are then seen through. You realize that you are timeless, spaceless, conscious love. In this realization, fall all the way through until what was first seen to be emptiness within is in fact realized as emptiness everywhere, inside and out. Silence within is realized to be silence as totality. The body and its thinking are seen to be a tiny speck within that.

Silent conscious love is the substratum of being. When you first catch a glimpse, it seems that it is inside of you.

As you continue to surrender to the enormity of the unknown, you realize that you are a speck of dust within It. If you then surrender into a deeper unknown, the speck of dust disappears, and your true nature dawns.

Then you are naturally a True Friend. Whoever meets you, meets their own heart of endless love. The more silent you are internally, the more you shine externally, and the world is lit by your grace.

This is the role of the True Friend.

If you have not yet realized yourself as the silent ground of being, give yourself fully without delay. No postponement is necessary or needed. Not so that you will get something or have a tool to use, and not as defeat or giving up, but rather the bold willingness to take a stand and surrender everything. When you give yourself fully, you are poured back into yourself in the fathomless depth of love.

If you give yourself to get something in the future, your samadhi, or experience of bliss, will be fleeting, and you will find yourself chasing after more. But if you are willing to be a servant of truth instead of the master of your world, you will find yourself in truth. Then you are a True Friend.

Until then, you can be willing in every moment of meeting an apparent other to have a quiet mind and an open heart and to be still and available. Then you are acting like a True Friend, in not acting at all. In this, the purity of the inside is in alignment with the openness on the outside.

To be your true self, Sat-Chit-Ananda in Sanskrit, is to be a Silent(Chit), Loving (Ananda), Being (Sat). As a teacher, therapist, guide, mentor, coach, partner, parent, or child, when sitting with a silent mind and an open heart, we are naturally emanating silent loving consciousness. In the moment when there is no grasping, running from, or defending, the veil of the ego disappears. Then the transparency of who you truly are shines with the light of the love of your heart in all its purity and clarity.

These are the fruits of being willing to be a True Friend. The techniques, exercises, or whatever else you may find useful in this book, have no substance without the power of being a True Friend. As a True Friend, everything will be useful. To be a True Friend is to be mentally silent with an open heart and to not move.

To be quiet enough and open enough means not to move with the habitual movement of your egoic "fixation." In general, mental fixations tend to move away in fear, emotional fixations move towards in neediness, and the anger fixations move against in rage. These are the general styles with some strong variations, as you will discover.

An important key is not to be fooled by the outer superficial behavior, but to see the deeper motivations that give rise to the behaviors.

To be a True Friend, you must have a quiet mind and an open heart, which means not taking anything personally. The wonderful mystery about being a True Friend is that in order to be a True Friend, you have to get out of the way. You must be transparent. When you show up as a somebody with something to say, you take up too much room, and there is no space to fully receive the other. When we are taking something personally, we are suffering in some way and clouding the purity of insight. When we are not taking anything personally, we are open and free.

To be a True Friend you have to be willing to not show up as a particular somebody, and to have self-control. As nobody in particular, there is no need to teach or impart your wisdom and insights. To be a True Friend is to be so empty that you can be present with whatever appears without having it impact you. You do not need to perform or prove or justify your existence.

You don't have to respond. You don't have to improve. You don't have to change. You don't have to fix. You don't have to justify your existence.

This is the rarest gift that we can give one another! The role of a True Friend is to model the possibility of not reacting to what passes before it, but rather to reflect it.

It is very useful to recognize the tendency to react. Then there can be a choice to use the arising of the tendency as a signal to relax and to rest ever more deeply in the truth of yourself.

Basic Principles of a True Friend

Let's assume a few basic principles to guide this process.

The first one, from Bandler and Grinder, (the co-founders of Neuro-Linguistic Programming) is that there is no failure, only feedback. In other words, there is no way to do it wrong. This is a process of learning and discovering, and the ideal context for learning is when you allow yourself and others the freedom to make mistakes. When you are not judging or comparing yourself to someone else or some idea of perfection, you can simply be open to the feedback you get and learn from it. You may even find you can deeply enjoy the process.

Most of us have learned that we are rewarded by giving the "right answer" or by performing some task "perfectly." We live in a society that values and rewards skills and qualities that serve the outer dimensions of our experience, but which mostly ignore or give little value to the discovery and experience of the inner depths of our Being. For being successful in the outer world, perhaps it is advantageous to cover up our inner sense of inadequacy or our fear of not knowing. But we are not here to know the right answer or to master a set of particular skills. Our true purpose in coming together is to allow ourselves to be seen, as we are, that we may more deeply uncover our true nature.

The basic skills we will be learning are simply a support for creating a context in which we can investigate, discover, and explore. A sincere desire to realize the truth and a willingness to experience whatever is really here is all that is needed. If you let go of the need to be perfect and right, the need to know what to say and what to do, then you will discover that you are delightfully free to make "mistakes" and learn from them. You will realize in your own experience that there is no failure, only feedback. You can then be spontaneous.

You can rest in your Self and be truly available to listen deeply. You can trust something deeper than the conscious mind and be unknowing and curious. You can be simple, easy, and natural. You can relax.

The second principle is that everyone has all the resources they need already.

Whoever you are working with is already perfect wisdom and infinite love itself, regardless of what they may tell you or try to convince you of. Wisdom and love itself needs nothing added to it. It is already perfect and complete.

Your role as a True Friend is simply to be the context in which they can discover the truth for themselves.

First recognize for yourself that the perception of being a "someone who needs something" is false–that it is just a trance induction masking the reality.

Once you have realized who you are, you will know the true identity of everyone you meet.

One of the great poisons in the world of therapy is the belief that the therapist has something that you don't, which they can give to you. If the therapist can give you something that you don't have, even if it is wonderful, the presupposition is that you are needy and incomplete. This type of relationship reinforces the belief that who you are is inherently deficient and in need of something. It reinforces the illusion in egoic identity.

The possibility is to expose to yourself this deep wound of deficiency and to meet it fully. In that you realize that deeper than any feeling or belief is the realization that you are wisdom and love itself and that you have all the resources you need already. Then naturally you will reflect this understanding to whomever you are with. Not by teaching or preaching what you have discovered, but by simply being who you are.

FINAL PRINCIPLE

An additional principle of this work is that you can only guide someone else to the depth you have realized yourself. Being truly effective in the role of a True Friend comes from the depth of your own realization. If you are realizing the peace and love of true Being, this is your transmission to others. If you are imagining yourself to be separate, afraid, and in need of love, then this is what you are transmitting regardless of how skilled or experienced you may be. This is why the essence of our time together is for you to have the opportunity to discover your own depth, rather than just learning and applying a set of techniques. Technique and skillfulness can be very useful, they can be a great support. There is no problem with technique. But in the role of the True Friend, technique can never be a substitute for realizing your own depth of Being.

Model of a True Friend:

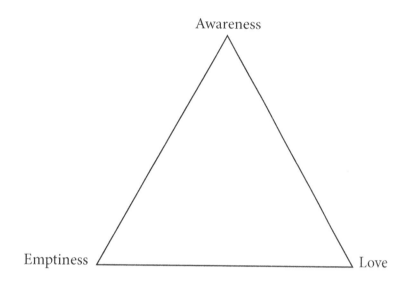

Awareness: Being aware of what is going on with whoever you are with.

Emptiness: Internally quiet, no internal dialogue, no knowing, judgements or opinions.

Love: Naturally arises in Awareness and Emptiness.

If you directly realize yourself as this model, and that is all that you get from reading this book, it would really be enough. In order to be a True Friend the only requirements are that you are aware, meaning being aware of what is going on with whoever is in front of you; empty, meaning internally quiet, no internal dialogue, no knowing, and out of that, love will naturally shine.

I have seen many therapists who show a lack of awareness and lack of emptiness. Instead there can be thinking, knowing, or relating by taking it personally. The client speaks and the immediate thought is, "Yes, I know what you are talking about."

"That must mean you fit in this category."

Or, "I know what you mean, that happened to me." There are different ways of reacting to what is presented: comparing, judging, personalizing, relating with, fixing or internally categorizing. All of these are strategies of the ego to try and control and as such are the noise that clouds clear awareness. The other extreme is the detached observer who mechanically reflects back.

If all you get from this book is this model of inquiry: of having a quiet mind, not knowing, being aware, and in love–then miracles will happen. All our conditioning, all of our training is to know the answer, to know what to do. From the time you were just a little baby you were rewarded for knowing and doing the right thing, for being good. All our training has been to know. This has been, and is, a very useful survival strategy. Knowing is not wrong, but it is limited in the context of serving another.

What I am challenging you to do is to not know; to give up all theoretical and conceptual knowing. There is going to be a tendency to compare what you are reading to what you already know, to what you have heard before, to what you have read somewhere, to make a note of it so that you can remember it later.

Forget all of that. There is no need for it. You will find that if you are not comparing, you are not talking to yourself, then what you hear and see in front of you has a chance to sink in to someplace deeper. To sink in and touch a place of empty wisdom. Talking to yourself creates a noise barrier to receiving on a deeper level.

If you live in and as awareness, emptiness, and love you will naturally be a True Friend to everyone you meet. The challenge is to be a True Friend for the world. Often it is easier to be empty aware love while in the role of the therapist or True Friend, but then when the session is over and your roles change, there is often the tendency to get involved with the suffering of "my life."

As well as skillful means of trance induction and intervention, we are going to discover how you leave being a True Friend and pick up the trance of **me**. Pick up, "My needs, and my issues," and, "What about me?" or, "I'm not getting mine," and you shift into the mode of suffering.

My intention is that everybody wake up and stay awake. You can play any role: therapist, father, son, mother, daughter, housewife, doctor, waitress, mailboy, secretary, or gardener. Wherever you are, you can be a True Friend for the world when you are empty and quiet, aware and in love. This is what we have all wanted, what we have all been praying for. The possibility of a world of harmony and peace, a world that is in balance.

All form is a trance. Fundamentally, nothing exists except pure consciousness. What we are seeing is Consciousness playing with Itself in the imagination of form. This is "maya," the veils that cover true essence with the forms of a world. Maya is a trance-induction. In this trance induction there is a possibility of heaven and the egoic suffering of hell. Now we are here to be heaven on earth.

The Three Movements of Ego

- **Movement Against**: When the egoic identity is crystallized in the physical body there is an impulse to anger, to control, to being right, to pushing against. *No* is the statement.
- **Movement Towards**: When the movement is crystallized in the emotional body there is an impulse to enter rapport, to win favor and approval. *Yes* is the statement of *I need*.
- **Movement Away**: When the tendency is crystallized in the mental body there is an impulse to pull away, to dissociate from the physical and emotional bodies, to think about what to do. *I doubt* is the underlying statement of fear.

Everyone you work with will be demonstrating these tendencies. The story of personal suffering is an account of the tendency to react to experience, rather than reflecting it. The role of the True Friend is to model the possibility of not reacting automatically, but of reflecting upon what appears with a quiet mind and open heart.

It is very useful to clearly recognize this tendency to react. Then there is the choice to use the arising of the tendency as a signal to not move.

Exercises for being aware of
the tendency to react

TOWARD, AWAY, AND AGAINST EXERCISES

Exercise A:

Part I
This exercise is done in silence, with eye contact, but no physical contact.

- Begin sitting–facing a partner.
- While the True Friend has a quiet mind, the partner has the experience of discovering what it feels like to move *away*. Notice the thinking required and the story to make the other a threat. *"Why are they invading my space?" for example.*
- True Friends note their own tendency to react to the client, and don't move.
- The partner can notice what has to do be done, mentally and emotionally in order to move in this way. You may notice whether this is easy or difficult to do, whether this is familiar or not.
- Shake it off and come back to Stillness and Emptiness.
- Maintaining the same roles and instructions, the client next has the experience of moving physically *towards*.
- Maintaining the same roles and instructions, the client has the experience of moving physically *against.*

Part II
- Switch roles and repeat Part I.

Part III
- Both let roles fall away and take a moment to experience each other without moving against, away or toward. Find the possibility of not moving. Be still in Awareness, Emptiness, and Love.

Part IV
- Take some time to share what you realized.

Exercises for being aware of the tendency to react

TOWARD, AWAY, AND AGAINST

Exercise B:

Repeating questions done in pairs

Part I:

- True Friend first asks their partner which tendency they would like to examine (perhaps "away" for fear points, "against" for anger points, etc.)

- Question #1:
  Who or what do you move away from? (or against or toward)

- Question #2:
  How do you move away from? (or against or toward)

- Question #3:
  Why do you move away from? (or against or toward)

Part II
- Switch roles and repeat Part I.

Part III
- Both let roles fall away and take a moment to experience each other without moving against, away or toward. Find the possibility of not moving. Be still in Awareness, Emptiness, and Love.

Part IV
- Take some time to share what you realized.

A word is a trance induction

Every word is a sound that refers to a personal, subjective, sensory specific experience. A word is a trance induction. A word triggers a different trance state in every person. The tendency is to assume that you know what is meant when someone uses a word to refer to an experience. When in the role of the therapist, rather than interpreting what is said, you can offer the gift of reflective awareness and discover what it is that is truly wanted and what is being experienced now, in sensory specific detail.

Any question is a trance induction! Any statement is a trance induction, because the person must go inside and make meaning out of it. But what we will discover in learning the principles of hypnosis, is that you can phrase your statements and questions in such a way that you can enter rapport with your client.

Excellent exercise:

- Write *excellent* in the center of the page, draw a circle around the word and place nine spokes coming off the circle. On each spoke write down what "excellent" means.
- Join with others in a small group of four or five. Appoint a scorekeeper. The scorekeeper draws four or five vertical columns on a sheet of paper representing the number of people agreeing to what excellent means.
- The first person in the group begins by reading the first word in their list of words. If no one else in the group had that word written down, then the scorekeeper makes a hash mark in column 1. If there are two matches record a hash mark in column 2, and so on. Don't record the word, only how many people had the exact same word. Each time a word is read everyone who has it on the list crosses it off so it will not be duplicated later on.
- After everyone has read their list, tally the columns to find out how much agreement there is on what *excellent* means.

Before this exercise, you may have thought, "I know what excellent means." Now you have discovered that your meaning is personal and refers to your own set of associations, pictures and sensations. So when a client says, "I want to have a good relationship." And you think, "I know what a good relationship is," you know now that this is your own trance.

So, what if you don't know, and you are simply willing to discover what is in front of you?

Two Sets of Questions

Form new partnerships. One will be the True Friend and ask the first set of questions and see where it leaves you mentally, physically, and emotionally. And then take the same issue and use the second set of questions and notice where that leaves you. And then we switch.

1. **Blame**
   What is wrong?
   How does it limit you?
   Whose fault is it?
   What should be done?

2. **Reframe**
   What do you want?
   How can this be an opportunity?
   What will it give you?
   What if you already had that?

The Components of the trance of "Me"

There are three major instincts or drives:

From our essential humanness we inherit the three major animal drives. These drives or instincts are the juices our organism runs on as it faces the relentless flow towards death. Death is not an instinct but an inevitable end of the organism in its present formation. These animal drives are present in all animals and directly relate to the first three chakras in the Hindu Yogic system.

- First Chakra: The home of the Self-Preservation instinct
- Second Chakra: The home of the Sexual instinct
- Third Chakra: The home of the Social Instinct

There are four bodies of manifestation:
- Physical: The home of behaviors
- Emotional: The home of feelings
- Mental: The home of thoughts
- Situational: The arena of one's life circumstances.

Together, the bodies create a bubble of perception. Each body is fed by the five senses, creating a sensory impression.

The five senses:
- Visual: seeing apparent external objects in awareness, and seeing internal visual impressions, remembered or created.
- Auditory: hearing external sounds in awareness, and hearing internal sounds and voices, remembered or created.

- Kinesthetic: the feeling of sensations and emotions.
- Olfactory: smelling externally, or internally remembered or created.
- Gustatory: tasting externally, or internally remembered or created.

The culmination of the blending of these senses creates a story that explains the present moment and is perfectly reflected in the situational body. This story is told through inner dialogue and inner vision of the mental body blending with the moods and feelings of the emotional body and the behaviors and attitudes of the physical body. This is the fundamental state of trance that we live in. We believe our own stories and act as if we have no control in making them up. We think they are not made up but "Reality!" Our possibility is the possibility of waking up.

2. RAPPORT *and* NLP

The therapist's job is to enter rapport with the client. In order to enter rapport, you can't bring your own baggage along with you. If you are empty and aware; if you don't know anything in particular but are curious; you can then enter rapport with the client's trance. If at any point rapport is broken, then the job of the therapist is to re-enter rapport.

I learned this invaluable lesson from Leslie Cameron Bandler in a certification program for NLP. Before learning by watching and modeling Leslie, I always just assumed I was in rapport. In fact, I was usually imposing my view on another.

Often the therapist expects the client to enter rapport. The client is expected to enter the therapist's story or version of what is happening. If the client experiences something different from what is expected or has another point of view or is confused or confrontational the client is often subtly blamed and called resistant. Your job as the therapist is to be able to enter the client's trance. To enter the client's trance, you must drop your own. It's that simple.

Rapport is the beginning, middle, and end of successful therapy. You can know the absolute truth, you can be the truth, you can know what the client needs, but without rapport, you will not be successful. With rapport, you don't have to know anything. You discover that the client has his or her own innate wisdom. The client his or herself is wisdom, covered with layers of trance. If you are in rapport, you can cut through the layers of trance, directly to wisdom. Clients can discover they have everything they need.

45

Rapport starts with trusting yourself. And what you will find is that trusting yourself leads to relaxation. As you relax, your mind gets quiet. As your mind gets quiet, you sink inside. As you sink inside, you find that you don't really need trust because you are already here.

EXAMPLE OF RAPPORT

In the early days of my practice in San Francisco I had someone come in whose presenting problem was that her boss was tapping her phone. My first response was to tell her to never call me from her home phone. (This was before cell phones.) This insured that her boss could not tap our conversations. We entered rapport and the work was very successful.

Your clients are going to come to you, for the most part, wanting a better dream. No problem, you can help them get a better dream. You will find that even in helping them get a better dream, the seeds can be planted for what is beyond the dream: the possibility of waking up. Some of your clients will come to you because they are ready to end the dream. In which case, the secret is this:

It is not how deep the client can go, it is how deep the therapist is.

You can only take your client as deep as you are. This is the key to successful therapy. So often I see therapists preach wonderful concepts to their clients, but they are just that–concepts. Concepts that the therapist believes in, and as concepts are just another burden to be overcome. Whether the concept is of love or God or unity or compassion, it is just another idea with no real weight. When insight comes from within the client as a direct realization from their own experience than it can be rooted in certainty that is beyond belief.

Components of Rapport

Rapport is an atmosphere of comfort, trust and understanding.
It underlies all mutually successful interactions.

Pacing is matching or mirroring the other person's verbal and non-verbal behavior. When it is done well it offers the other person a feedback loop, where their inner state is reflected back to them clearly with minimal distortion. This is a very important and effective element in entering rapport. If pacing is done too mechanically, or without awareness, the other person may feel like they are being mimicked and rapport may be lost. Although it is essentially simple, pacing is an art as well as a skill. Good pacing offers the other the experience of feeling understood, truly listened to and being heard.

Pacing–matching and mirroring:

- Posture: Basic position, tempo of movement, gestures (without mimicking)
- Breathing: Tempo, location
- Vocal Qualities: Tempo, rhythm, pitch, tone, loudness
- Verbal Predicates: Sensory Modes: Visual, Auditory, Kinesthetic

Cross-Modal Matching or Cross-Over Mirroring:

Matching a person but with a different type of behavior

- Pacing breathing with hand movements
- Pacing the vocal qualities with facial expression
- Pacing breathing with vocal qualities

Other components of rapport:

Intention for service: caring, interested, and able.

Reflective Validations: Reflecting back their statements, feelings, intentions, their predicaments or situation.

Exercise for entering Rapport

PACING WORDS EXACTLY:

Pacing, or matching and mirroring, is a very effective way of entering rapport. A very simple way to experience this, is to pace someone's words exactly. The tendency when someone says something, is to interpret what is said, make your own internal associations, then feed back your words about what was just said.

When this happens, the client has to go inside and find his or her own meaning for the words you have used. They have to enter your trance.

If instead you give them back their words exactly, using the same tone of voice they use, they can have the experience of having what they said and how they said it, reflected back to them. By simply being aware of what is said, and feeding it back without altering it, the client can have the experience of feeling heard, and "understood." Pacing is an art; if done without awareness the person you are pacing may feel parroted or mimicked; if done with awareness and love in a context where it is appropriate, you are offering a gift of reflective presence.

PACING EXERCISE:

- Have your partner make a statement. Perhaps about something they are experiencing.
- Feed it back slightly differently. Perhaps changing a few words and saying it with a slightly different intonation.
- Next, feed it back word for word and in the same tone. Repeat this step if you need to, until your partner confirms that you matched them.
- Notice the difference. When your pacing is successful, it will be obvious to you both.

Predicates

MATCHING LANGUAGE MODALITIES:

Exercise:

- Your partner tells a story about a noteworthy incident, perhaps from work. You encourage the story by asking questions and reflecting back their statements.
- Note the predicates they use when telling the story, and speak in the same modality (visual, auditory, or kinesthetic) when responding with questions and reflected statements.
- At some point, experiment with mismatching the predicates by using a different modality in questions or statements and note the results.
- Take some time to discuss what you discovered with your partner.

Components of Sensory Input

- **Sensory Experience** - the combined impressions of the five senses:
  Visual, Auditory, Kinesthetic, Olfactory, and Gustatory:
  What is seen, what is heard, what is felt, what is smelled, and what is tasted.

- **Memories**:
  These are past impressions of sensory experience that are stored internally as pictures, sounds, feelings, smells, and tastes.

- Dissociated Memories:
  These are when you see yourself from a distance in the scene.

- Associated Memories:
  These are when you have the experience of being in your body then, and seeing the scene out of your eyes as you saw it then.

  Associated Memories usually include all the sense modes, especially the kinesthetic, while dissociated memories are primarily visual in most cases.

Cues for modes of thinking

VISUAL THINKING:

- Eye movements: up and left, up and right, and/or straight ahead with dilated pupils.
- Head position: head tilted upward
- Breathing: high in the chest; shallow or cessation of breathing
- Voice tempo: quick bursts of words; rapid tempo
- Tone of voice: high-pitched, nasal
- Skin color: pale
- Muscle tension: tight, high shoulders, tense abdomen

AUDITORY THINKING:

- Eye movements: down and left, level and right, level and left
- Head position: level, tilted left, turned so one ear toward speaker
- Breathing: even breathing with the whole chest
- Voice tempo: rhythmic breathing
- Tone of voice: melodic, resonant
- Skin: even coloring
- Muscle Tension: rhythmic, even movements and tension

KINESTHETIC THINKING (body sensations and feelings):

- Eye movements: down and right
- Head Position: below the horizontal, tilted to the right

- Breathing: deep breathing low in the stomach
- Voice tempo: slow tempo, long pauses
- Tone of voice: low, deep, breathy
- Skin color: increased, flushed
- Muscle Tension: muscle relaxation, sudden movements.

3. Discovering *the* Present Condition

The Present Condition is one's present experience and realization. It includes the mental, emotional and physical state that they are presently experiencing and would like to change or examine – as well as their depth of realization of who they really are (Awareness, Emptiness, Love) which is transcendent to all states.

The Present Condition usually includes a state of mind/body/emotion that occurs more strongly in a particular context and is often triggered by a particular signal or stimulus (visual, auditory or kinesthetic). The mental/emotional state that is presented is a trance induction. Which means that it is not real, but yet it seems real. What makes it seem so real is that all of the bodies (mental, emotional and physical), and most of the senses (esp. visual, auditory, kinesthetic) are involved in some way.

Some are more conscious and obvious, and some are running more subconsciously and are overlooked. Bringing the whole structure of this state into conscious awareness begins to defuse the power of this trance state.

Questions, which help to clarify sensory-based descriptions, together with feeding back or pacing partners' responses appropriately, is a very effective way to discover the Present Condition.

Discovering the Present Condition:

- Find some situation or response that is undesirable in some way. True Friend can help your partner discover how this experience is put together:

  Externally: What is seen and heard in the situation?
  What is the trigger?

  Internally: What is happening mentally?
  What are the submodalities of pictures and dialogue?
  What is happening physically and emotionally?
  In what order do you have these experiences?

The Structure of Thinking

Generally our attention is on the content of the thought, and not on the structure. seeing the structure of thinking allows us to see how we do it, how we suffer, or how we create our reality or our experience. In seeing it, insight can come naturally. Certain processes and structures fall away when they are seen to not be useful.

EXERCISE:

Part A: What does thinking mean?

- True Friend: Help your partner to discover what they mean when they say they are thinking about something.

  Are they seeing images and movies? If so, where do they see them? How big are the pictures? Is it black and white or color? What other distinctions can you make?

  Are they hearing an inner dialogue? If so, where is the voice located? Whose voice is it? What is the tone or emotional quality of the voice?

  Perhaps thinking means to them that they are primarily experiencing body sensations and feelings that have some personal meaning. If so, what are these feelings? Where are they experiencing them? What specifically do they mean?

- In a really good trance, thinking will mean a combination of images, words, sounds, sensations and feelings that happen in a way that is so familiar that we call the experience "me." Discover the different components that are involved in your partner's mode of thinking.

- To ensure accuracy and offer your partner the experience of feeling understood, the True Friend can reflect back to their partner in the partner's own words, what has just been discovered.

Part B: Examining the apparent "need" for thinking.

- True Friend: Help your partner to discover the positive intention of "thinking", and to examine whether it is really needed to fulfill this intention. Many will find that this line of inquiry may relax any struggle with the thinking process, and may deepen trust in one's Essence.

- What is the positive intention of "thinking"?

- Do you really need to "think" in order to fulfill this intention?

- What are you afraid would happen if you didn't "think" about "it?"

- What is the truth of your experience about this?

- Who is having this internal dialogue, making pictures and having feelings about them? Who is this?

The Structure of Emotion

Similarly to thought, our emotions have a structure. We relate them to stories, thoughts and identity. We create a meaning out of it, and in that way, they become entrenched and form subconscious patterns. To see the structure of emotions, new insights become available and choice is here to change the structure and change the pattern to see through it.

EXERCISE: WHAT DOES ANGER MEAN? (OR SADNESS, FEAR, ETC.)

Part A: Discovering the Structure of Emotion

- True Friend: Discover what your partner's experience of an emotion is.
  What is going on mentally? (visual or auditory)
  What is happening in the body? What sensations are felt and where?
  In what order do these things happen?
- To ensure accuracy and offer your partner the experience of feeling understood, the True Friend can demonstrate the loop: from the first signal that triggers the emotion, through the mental, physical and emotional bodies, in whatever order they happen for your partner.

Part B: Acknowledging the Positive Intention

- True Friend: Help your partner to discover what the positive intention is of the emotion they are experiencing and to examine whether it is really needed to fulfill this intention. Here are some possible questions to explore this:
- What is the positive intention of feeling angry (sad, afraid etc.)?

- Is it necessary to feel this emotion in order to fulfill this intention?
- What do you think would happen if you didn't feel angry (or sad or afraid) about "it?"
- What is the truth of your experience about this?
- Who is having this internal dialogue, making pictures and having feelings about them? Who is this?

The Nesting of Emotions

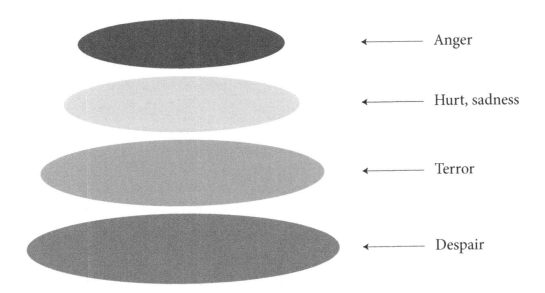

← Anger

← Hurt, sadness

← Terror

← Despair

Emotions are limited. They have a beginning, a middle and an end. Generally, when feeling a negative emotion, there is a sense of it being endless, so we stay above them. We try to suppress them, avoid them, resist them and distract from them. We tell a story about them as a way to dissociate from them.

Most people live in superficial emotions, and create a story about themselves or others or the world as a way to avoid the deeper emotions. To bring awareness to these levels of emotions can bring a clarity and profound insight into what is really going on at a deeper level.

If you are willing to plunge into any emotion; if you are willing to say, "Okay, it is a good day to die, come and get me," and then dive in, you can discover that underneath each emotion, is another emotion. And under that emotion, is another one.

This particular illustration of the Nesting Pattern of Emotions is true for most people, but not all. You will find that some people are wired differently.

The enneagram provides a map for the different fixations and how their emotions are nested. For Nines, the most surface emotion is not anger, it is sadness. Under sadness there is usually fear. It is much easier for a Nine to feel sadness and fear than it is to feel anger.

For a Nine to get in to anger, it is very close to despair, very close to the explosion of hopelessness. This is also true for certain self-preservation Sixes, because for the Six to feel anger could be dangerous for survival. Many Sixes who mistake themselves for nines, say, "I don't get angry, I am helpful." Helpfulness is a way of staying safe. Anger becomes suppressed and is closer to despair.

You will also find that it is possible to drop from anger directly into essence. It is possible to drop from sadness and hurt directly into essence. Or from fear into essence.

The key is don't act on it and don't suppress it. This is really the revolutionary news. Because, basically, all of our lives, we have been taught to either act it out or suppress it. Either it is not appropriate to feel this, or "I shouldn't feel this so I will make believe it's not here."

In establishing the present condition, often the emotion that is most surface, the one that the client is reporting, is covering another deeper emotion that is more relevant, and more essential to understand the true presenting condition.

When the client is asked what is underneath that emotion, it can illicit an insight or realization. "Oh, I'm not actually afraid, I'm feeling hurt." Or "I'm not really angry, I'm actually scared!" This can unlock a pattern, or at the very least allow the session to be more direct and relevant to what is really going on for the client.

Submodalities

- **Visual**
  Associated or dissociated perspective
  Framed or panoramic
  Color or black and white
  Brightness
  Size of picture
  Distance of picture from self
  3-dimensional or flat
  Moving or still
  Focused or unfocused
  Angle of view

- **Auditory**
  Volume
  Tempo
  Rhythm
  Inflection
  Pauses
  Tonality
  Resonance
  Location
  Words, voice

- **Kinesthetic**
  Temperature
  Weight
  Pressure
  Location
  Texture
  Movement
  Steady or Intermittent

Submodalities of a Memory

I. Discover the visual, auditory, and kinesthetic submodalities of an unpleasant memory.
- Is the memory associated or dissociated?
  (If it is associated, then have them dissociate from it ... seeing it from a distance.)
- What are the submodalities of what is seen?
- What are the submodalities of what is heard?
- What are the submodalities of what is felt?

II. Discover the visual and auditory and kinesthetic submodalities of a pleasant memory.
- Is the memory associated or dissociated?
  (If it is dissociated, then have them fully associate with it ... experiencing it, as if fully in the body, experiencing it the way you did then)
- What are the submodalities of what is seen?
- What are the submodalities of what is heard?
- What are the submodalities of what is felt?

Changing Submodalities Exercise

1. Have your partner enter a pleasant memory. Change the submodalities and notice the experience.
2. Make the memory brighter and notice. Make it larger. Add motion and sound. intensify feelings, bring in smells. One at a time and notice.
3. Next take a negative memory and do the same things. Change size to smaller this time, add distance, change from color to black and white. Experiment and discover that happens to an experience when the submodalities change.
4. Try moving the voice in your partner's head to the other side. Change the tone, the speed, the rhythm without changing the content and notice each modality change and its effect.

Information Gathering

INTRODUCTION TO THE META-MODEL:

The Meta-Model was developed by Bandler and Grinder as a map of the structure of language and meaning. It is not necessary to memorize the Meta-Model to be an effective communicator and therapist. The essence of good information gathering is to not "know" what "excellent" means; to not assume you know what the client means by the words they use. The meta-model gives us the structure of what we tend to overlook in hearing another's story of their experience.

The purpose of learning the meta-model is to give you mastery at discovering the Desired State and the Present State. Once the meta-model has been internalized, you will intuitively use these principles in an elegant way.

The meta-model is a set of linguistic information-gathering tools designed to reconnect a person's language to the experience that is represented by their language. Language is not the experience, but rather a representation of visual, auditory, and kinesthetic experience, as a map is a representation of a territory.

Essentially, the Meta-Model serves as an interface between language and experience. Human behavior makes sense when it is seen in the context of the choices generated by a person's map or model. We create our models of what we call *reality* through three universal human modeling processes.

1. Generalization:

The process by which components or pieces of a person's model of the world become detached from their original experience, and come to represent the entire category of which the experience is an example.

2. Deletion:

The process by which we selectively pay attention to certain aspects of our experience and exclude others.

3. Distortion:

The process that allows us to make shifts in how we experience sensory data.

The Meta-Model

- **QUESTION SOFTENERS**:
  "Please tell me … "
  "I'm wondering … "
  "I'm curious to know … "
  "I'm not sure what you mean … "
  "I wonder if you could help me understand … "

  CAUTION! If you ask for information or challenge what someone is saying without using Softeners, this request for more information can seem like an *attack* to the other person, and rapport may be lost.

- **UNSPECIFIED NOUNS**:
  When a person, place or thing is introduced into a sentence but not specified, request that a noun or noun phrase be specified further to obtain relevant and deleted information: What specifically? Who, specifically? Where specifically?

  "The rules are too rigid here."
  ""I'm wondering which rules, specifically, are too rigid?"
  "I have too many things to do at once!"
  "What, in particular, do you have to do now?"

- **UNSPECIFIED VERBS**:
  The verb is introduced but not clarified leaving us in the dark about the experience. Asking the verb specification reconnects the person more fully to his

experience. To request for more specifics on how an action is to be performed or, for example, what that action is, ask: How, specifically?

"We must improve customer service."

"I'm curious, how specifically, can we improve service?"

"They were very rude." ("stupid," "silly," etc.)

"How, in particular, were they rude?"

- **UNIVERSALS:**
Refer to the set of words: All, every, always, never, nobody.
Request to look more closely at a generalization and a search for counterexamples to that generalization: "Was there ever a time?"

"I'm always nervous when people ask me questions."

"Always? Has there ever been a time when you weren't?"

"I never am able to be comfortable saying 'no' to others. "

"Never? Is there any circumstance where you are?"

- **LIMITS:**
Impossibility: ("can't", "unable,", "incapable")

Necessity: ("should," "shouldn't," "must," "ought," "need," "have to")

A request for the specific conditions that make an action either necessary or impossible: "What stops you?" "What would happen if you … " "I can't do that"

"What stops you?" "What would it be like if you could?"

"I should know the answers."

"I'm wondering what would happen if you didn't know the answer?"

- **COMPARISONS:**
A request for the standard or object which is being compared to: "Better, Worse, More than what?"

"It's better to act like you know the answers."

"Better than what?"

"I want to be more calm and cool."

"More than what?"

- **REFERENCE:**
A request for the source of information or evaluation: "According to whom?" "For whom?"

"I shouldn't bend the rules."
  "According to whom?"
"It's better to give an answer immediately, even if you don't know."
  "Better for whom?" "According to whom?"

- **NOMINALIZATIONS:**
Words that have been transformed from process verbs into nouns. To transform a nominalization back into a process word, use it as a verb in response.

"I want to have a relationship. "
  "Are you relating with me now?"
"I want to have more success in my life.
  "In what areas would you like to succeed? "
"I want to release my anger."
  "What are you angry about?"

- **COMPLEX EQUIVALENCE**:
A generalization between two events that are unrelated in reality.
This is expressed as X = Y.

  "How do you know X means Y?"
"My husband never appreciates me … my husband never smiles at me."
"Help me understand. Does your husband's not smiling at you always mean that he doesn't appreciate you?"

- **MIND READING:**
Belief that one person can know what another person is thinking or feeling without direct communication from that person.

  "How do you know?"
"He doesn't like me."
  "I'm wondering, how do you know he doesn't like you?

- **CAUSE AND EFFECT:**
  Belief that some action on the part of one person can cause another person to act in a particular way or to experience some emotion or inner state.

  X causes Y: "You make me sad."
  (External Behavior causes Internal State)

  Recover the Submodalities of X: How, specifically does X cause Y?
  "My wife makes me angry."
      "I'm curious what is it in your wife's behavior that makes you feel angry."

- **LOST PERFORMATIVE**: Bad, Good, Crazy, Sick
  Recover source of reference: Internal, External etc.
      According to whom?
  "I'm a bad person."
  "I'm curious to know according to whom are you a bad person?"

4. Discovering *the* Desired Condition

"What do you want?" This is the beginning point, and foundation of effective communication and inquiry. This is an essential question. When you are in the role of True Friend, if you do not first find out what someone is really wanting, then any attempt on your part to help or support will be coming from your desire and intention not theirs. Your job is to first help them to clearly discover what it is they really want.

Discovering the level of commitment is also essential: "What do you want and what are you willing to give for it?" Or, "What have you been unwilling to give?" Here you are inviting into awareness unconscious aspects of mind that have been invested in desiring something else. As they become conscious of how their desiring force has been diluted, these desires can now be examined to discover if they are getting the person what they really want.

When there is a clear intention, a strong desire and a total commitment to that intention, then whatever needs to be uncovered, seen, and experienced along the way, unfolds quite naturally.

Setting Explicit Outcomes and Intentions

What do you want? (desired state):

- State in positive terms
  (Not what they *don't* want, but rather what they *do* want).
- Initiated and controlled by the client
- Specific sensory-based description
- Appropriate chunk size

How will you know when you have it?

> *"What will you see?"*
> *"What will you hear?"*
> *"What will you be feeling?"*

Initiated and maintained by client:

Not dependent on the actions of others, such as "I don't want them to do that again."
> *"What stops you from having it?"*
> *"What do you need to do?"*
> *"How are you going to do it?"*
> *"What resources do you already have that will get what you want?"*

Contextualized:

> *"When do you want it?"*
> *"When do you not want it?"*
> *"Always?"* (generate counter-examples.)

Preserve positive byproducts:

> *"What are the disadvantages of having it?"*
> *"What are the advantages of the present state?"*

Ecological:

> *"Is there any part of you that doesn't want it?*

Exercise: Finding the Desired Condition: The True Friend helps their partner to discover what they want, and in what context they want to experience it:

What do you really want?
In what context do you want it? Where, when and with whom?
How will you know when you have what you want?
What will you be experiencing mentally, emotionally,
physically and essentially?
What will signal you when to have this experience?

Ecology

What is the positive function or value of the original behavior or response?

- Example:
Let's say that the Present State of how one performed a given task was "Nervous," and this means "making mistakes and being energetic."
Present State = mistakes, energetic

    A possible desired outcome might be to be "relaxed" while performing the same task. And let's say that "relaxed" means "not making mistakes, but it is boring."

    Possible Desired Outcome = no mistakes, but boring

    A Desired State which is Ecological would preserve the positive aspect of the original response, which is "energetic." This might be called "excited", and mean, "not making mistakes, and being energetic."

    Ecological Desired State = no mistakes, energetic

- Drinking, Smoking and Over-eating usually have a positive by-product:
Let's say it was "Relaxing when nervous."

    How else could you get this result? Ecological change preserves and addresses the positive function of the original behavior or response.

AS-IF

AS-IF is useful to establish a context where one is free to be resourceful, either in accessing Internal States or in gathering hidden Information. AS-IF takes a person into another context where that would be possible. When a person has entered the Resourceful context, he/she is freer to access desired states or information.

- Establishing As-If:

    The following are possible leads:

    "If you were to … what would that be like?"

    "Can you imagine a way in which you could?"

    "What would you experience if you already could … ?"

    "What if you were to act as if … "

    "Pretend that … "

- Switching Contexts:

    Person Switch: "If you were … ?" (someone else who can)

    Time Switch: "If it were six months down the road … ?"

    "Has there ever been a time when you could?"

    Function Switch: "If you could change anything, then … ?"

    Place Switch:

    "Is there a particular setting where you can experience that?"

    Dissociated and Curious: "What if you could see yourself discovering new ways to _____?"

Steering

The art of therapy is rooted in the therapist's capacity to steer. There are four directions in which to steer the client.

UP

You can steer up, which means taking the stated desire to a larger frame. For example, asking *what having that will do for you.*

DOWN

You can steer down into the senses and the submodalites. For example, *What would that feel like? Where is that located in your body?*

BACK

You can always go backwards in time.
Do you remember when … ?
Was there ever a time … ?
Has this happened before … ?

FORWARD

How will this change in the future when … ?
The next time … ?
When the circumstance reappears … ?

Steering up

DESIRES TO ESSENTIAL DESIRE

Examining desires

- First make a list of all your desires. Be sure to include the desires that are "not spiritual."
- Working with one desire at a time, the True Friend assists the partner in examining the deeper levels of desiring that are nested under it.

  Begin with any desire such as: "I want a good job" or, "I want a better relationship."

  True Friend acknowledges their desire:

  "That's right, you want a good job."

  Then asks one of the following questions:

  "And what will that get you?"

  Or, "What will having this do for you?"

  Or, "And if you had that experience, what is it that you want through having that?"

  Or, "If you have this, is there something you want that may be even more essential?"

- Continue this process of acknowledging each new desire that is uncovered and discovering why they want it. You will discover how desires are nested one inside the other. Keep going until a desire for an Essential State of Being is uncovered: such as peace, love, oneness, bliss. Allow them to fully experience this now.
- It can seem like one has to first fulfill a whole chain of desires in order to realize the peace or love or other aspects of Essence, but in truth they are always present and need no cause or condition to be. Recognizing the Essential Desire

within a whole nesting of conditional desires can bring new light to the situation. Previously it may have seemed that this original desire needed to be fulfilled in order to be happy. Now it can clearly be recognized that this desire does not need to be fulfilled, and True Essence or True Self (what is ultimately wanted) does not need anything in order to be realized now.

Steering Down

Working with spiritual materialism/chunking down

- It is common to desire Spiritual Realization or Essential States, in order to get something else for "me." In this case, rather than starting from conditional desires and working through to Essence, the starting point is the stated desire for freedom, enlightenment, realization, awakening etc.

    This uncovering of how the ego would like to use the realization of Truth for its own ends, allows for this aspect of mind to be examined, and for clearer seeing of what is really wanted ... regardless of how that may reflect in conditional experience and appearances.
- True Friend can ask with deep love and understanding:
    "If you were awake, (fully realized etc.), then what would that get for you?"
- Whatever egoic desires are uncovered can then be examined by taking them through the nesting.

For instance: "If I were awake, then everyone would love me."
True Friend: "And if everyone loved you, what would that get you?"
Partner: "Then I would be safe and taken care of."
True Friend: "And if you were safe and taken care of, what would that be like right now?"
Partner: "Then I could relax completely."
True Friend: "What would be going on physically?"
Where would you feel that?
What would be going on emotionally?
What would be going on mentally?

Anchoring The Desired Condition

Steps for Anchoring the Desired Condition

Step 1: Ask and invite the client to feel and **experience the Desired Condition fully**. E.g. *"Can you feel the deep peace through your whole body? What if you can let yourself feel it fully right now?"*

Step 2: **Ask permission** to touch their knee or shoulder, then with a medium level pressure, **touch their knee or shoulder at the same time as they are feeling the Desired Condition**. Note: It may be more appropriate to have them create their own anchor at this stage. In this case, you invite them to touch their own knee, or hand on their heart, or any other place on their body, again at the same time as they are feeling the Desired Condition.

Step 3: **Strengthen the anchor**. Invite the client to find a time in their memory when they had felt this feeling even stronger than they are feeling it now. If they can't find a memory of feeling this feeling even stronger, invite them to imagine they have, or make believe they have. Then squeeze the knee or have them make contact with their own anchor while they are feeling the Desired Condition even stronger than the first time you set the anchore.

Step 4: **Strengthen the anchor one more time.** This time invite them to imagine or find someone who can feel this Desired Condition even stronger than they can. Usually the client will be able to quickly find a person they imagine feels this feeling stronger than they can feel it. Then ask them to imagine they are inside this person's body, feeling what they feel. As you visibly confirm the strength of the Desired Condition is even stronger than the previous time, press their anchor or have them press their anchor again.

You can then test the anchor, by firing it again and seeing if it works effectively, or you can wait until the intervention stage when this anchor can be used to force the Desired Condition to arise in the client to support the client seeing their Present Condition in a different way and learning whatever lesson is needed to learn.

PART THREE

Hypnosis

1. INDUCTION

What Happens in Hypnosis

Ego Strengthening:

- The planning function of the conscious mind subsides.
- An increased sense of relaxation and comfort.
- An alert state–not sleep.
- A reduction of peripheral awareness.
- An increased vividness and intensity of internal experience: visual, auditory, and kinesthetic.
- An increased availability of imagery from the past.
- A heightened ability for creative imagination.
- An increased ability to dissociate from memories or internal experience that one is usually associated with.
- An increased ability to associate with memories and feelings that are usually dissociated.
- A reduction of reality testing and tolerance for persistent reality distortion.
- An increase in suggestibility.
- An increased ability to attend to, organize and appreciate human experience and learning potential.
- The accessing of abilities that are usually ignored or only marginally perceived during usual conscious processing and in typical daily actions.
- Enhancement of role behavior and modeling abilities.
- Partial or complete amnesias may occur.

Ego Transcendence:

- An ease in slipping out of the trance of the waking state.
- A natural subsidence of mind-activity.
- Increased capacity to experience essential states.
- Increased depth of certain classes of Samadhi.
- Increased capacity for surrender.

Entering Trance

First Trance: Discover what takes you deeper and what takes you out.

Triads or dyads:
- Have the person who will be entering "trance" remember and name a pleasurable activity. Only give the name without details.
- Client: Close your eyes and pretend that you are in trance.
  Relive the activity fully associated.
- True Friends: Take turns making statements with the intention to deepen the experience of the person in trance. Notice if each statement takes them deeper or not.
- After about ten minutes, switch positions.
- Each person has a turn to enter trance.
  Second Trance: Same as first trance, except, use the following:
- Pace breathing with voice.
- Be aware of rhythm and tone of voice.
- Bring in the senses (especially visual, auditory, and kinesthetic)
- Use non-specific nouns and verbs.
- Use softeners.

First Trance Discussion

We discovered in your first experiment of doing a trance induction, that there were certain things that helped your partner to go deeper, and certain things that seemed to bring them out. In doing the trance yourself you experienced that as well; what worked to take you deeper, and what worked to bring you out. Rhythm is important. If you can pace their rhythm, the trance goes deeper. If you go too fast, they get into their head. If you go too slowly maybe you will lose them.

You also discovered that it mustn't be too specific. If I tell you to imagine a balloon, and then tell you that it is green … maybe for you it is a red balloon. Then I am no longer in rapport with the trance you are experiencing. We found that by using nonspecific nouns and verbs, your partner can use that to discover their own experience. If I say it is an "excellent balloon", for you it can be an "excellent" balloon, because I am not telling you what an "excellent" balloon means. If you are nonspecific, the clients can find their own meaning and experience.

You also may have found that by bringing in all of the senses, this too helped to deepen the trance. And here again, bringing in the senses in a non-specific way. If you say to your partner, "You can see a blue sky with white clouds", you may be too specific. If you are imposing your trance on them, this may take them out. However, if you bring in the senses in a non-specific way, as in "Perhaps as you look at the sky its color can become more vivid", they will have to go inside to discover what the color is, and you are in rapport with your partner.

You may also find that pacing their breathing can help to deepen the trance. You can take some time to simply breathe in unison with your partner. This alone can be a very powerful way of entering rapport. You may also try speaking just during their exhale, and notice the effect.

What we are learning now is rapport skills. Learning what worked and what didn't work in pacing your partner to go deeper into their trance. You will find with a little practice it is very natural and easy.

Pacing and Leading into Trance

"What are you aware of now?"

- The True Friend begins by asking the partner: "What are you aware of now?"
- Partner responds. For example: "I am aware of the sounds in the room."
- True Friend offers validation, then matches words, rhythm and tone exactly: "That's right, you are aware of the sounds in the room"
- True Friend can then make a couple short additional statements that are verifiable in sensory awareness:

  "You may also be aware of … the sound of my voice, and the color of my shirt. The "color of my shirt" may demand that the client open his or her eyes and Interrupt the trance-state … and you might begin to notice a certain sensation in the soles of your feet … "
- True Friend uses the presupposition of cause and effect, to suggest that whatever is being experienced will cause them to more deeply enter trance. For example:

  "And all of this can take you deeper … " or,

  "And this can be a signal for everything to relax, as you sink deeper into trance …"
- True Friend begins the loop again: "What are you aware of now?"
- The partner's attention may begin focusing on more external realities. The True Friend can pace whatever they are aware of and lead their attention to more internal experience, and into the desired state of trance.
- After you have gone through the loop several times and your partner is in a comfortable state of trance, you might utilize the trance state in some way. Here is an example of a non-specific process instruction:

"There is an important lesson for you to learn right now … something very important for you to recognize at this time … allow yourself to be aware of this now … take the time you need now to realize this very important lesson … "

"What are you aware of now?" Discussion

What we have been working with is rapport. Now we are going to enter rapport, and do a trance induction with someone, using what we have learned so far. What we are going to do is set up a biofeedback loop. The True Friend, sitting in Emptiness and Awareness, simply asks the partner, "What are you aware of now?" And whatever they say, you agree with them. "That's right, you are aware of … " and you feed it back to them in their own words, their own rhythm, their own cadence.

Then you are going to add in a few other things that they must also be aware of but they may not mention. Like, "That's right, and you may also be aware of the sound of the birds, and the sensation of sitting on the floor, and your breathing … and all of this can take you deeper." And these things that you are suggesting will be linked together with the suggestion, "and all of this can take you deeper."

This is one of "Maya's" secrets, creating the appearance of cause and effect. One of Maya's operating principles is: "this" makes "that" happen. We are going to "homeo-pathically" use this same principle that Maya uses to create the trance of suffering–to slip out of the trance of "me" and into the depth of yourself.

Everyone has been tricked with this illusion of cause and effect. We may call it karma.

More examples of Inductions

These are some basic examples of trance inductions that can be used to assist the client going deeper into relaxation and into the trance state, preparing for the intervention.

1. Roman numerals I, II, III

Step 1: Invite the client to imagine a **Roman numeral number three** floating in front of them. Invite them to imagine that this number has a very special color, just for them, and a special vibration emanating from the Roman numeral, and that this color or light is just perfect to bring healing and rest to the physical body. Have it go through the body and imagine the cells of the body coming to rest.

Step 2: Invite them to imagine the Roman numeral number two in front of them now. This time it has another color and vibration, this time just perfect for the emotional body. This color and vibration brings healing and peace to the emotional body, in all the places where emotions have been stored.

Step 3: Invite them to imagine the Roman numeral number one now in front of them. This time it has another color and vibration, just right to bring peace to the client's mental body, to their nervous system. Have them feel the color and vibration emanating from the Roman numeral number one through their whole body, bringing peace and nourishment to the nerves and neurons of the body.

2. Numbers between 1 and 10

Step 1: Invite the client to imagine a number between 1 and 10, where the number represents their state of relaxation. You can have 10 being totally and deeply relaxed, and 1 being wide awake, or you can reverse them depending on what you prefer.

Step 2: Ask the client to name a number that best represents their state of relaxation. Use softeners like "*Now I don't know what number you are, and it doesn't really matter, but you can imagine right now a number arising, and can you tell me what number it is that you see?*"

Step 3: There are many variations on how you can proceed here. One option is to use the same structure of the colors and vibration healing the physical, emotional and mental bodies, with the number progressively going towards the more relaxed state. Another option is to ask them what number they would like to be at, and then invite them to let themselves feel whatever they need to feel to go to a deeper state of relaxation.

3. Basic Beach trance

Invite the client to imagine they are at their favorite beach. Have them go through all the modalities: kinesthetic (feeling), auditory (hearing), visual, etc. Ask them to feel the sand between their toes, hear the sounds of the waves, see the waves coming in and out, feel the sun on their skin, etc.

This can be a way to bring a client deeper into trance just by itself, and can serve as the entrypoint to an intervention.

Alternatively you can also do a version of the Roman numerals induction by having the client find a special stick on the ground, and to write the number 3 in the sand, and as they are writing it, they can feel a deep healing of the physical body. Then the waves come in and wash away the number 3, and they can write the number 2 in the sand, and so on. Many variations on this theme can work well.

The Milton Model
Hypnotic Language Patterns

The Meta-Model sets out to deconstruct the presenting trance of the client. The Milton Model is the mirror image of the Meta-Model and is used to induce trance states.

- **NOMINALIZATIONS:**
  Non-tangible nouns: turning a process word into a noun

  Examples: freedom, love, resources, curiosity, knowledge, clarity, difficulty, unconscious mind

  *"as you experience the comfort of **knowledge and clarity** ... "*

- **UNSPECIFIED VERBS:**
  Non-sensory-based verbs.

  Examples: experience, remember, notice, think, know, understand, change, wonder, become aware.

  *"I invite you to **experience** more of your memories as you **remember** what is appropriate and learn from the things that you **notice** are **important.**"*

- **UNSPECIFIED REFERENTIAL INDEX:**
  Noun is not specified.

  *"The **signs** are obvious." "**People** can relax." "**This** is good."*

- **DELETION:**
  A major noun phrase is completely missing.

  *"**It's** too much." "As you have **learned** so much."*

- **CAUSAL MODELING OR LINKAGE:**
  Words of cause and effect

  > **And:** *"You are listening to my voice, **and** you can begin to relax."*

  > **As, when** (Connections in Time):

  *"**As** you sit there smiling, you can begin to remember."*

  Makes: *"The nodding of your head will **make** you relax even more."*
  More, the more: The ***more** you breathe deeply, **the more** you begin to remember what is helpful to you …"*

- **MIND READING:** Acting as if you know the internal experience of the client.
  "You may be wondering what I will say next."

- **LOST PERFORMATIVE:**
  The person evaluating is lost.

  *"**It is not important** that you understand everything."*

- **UNIVERSAL QUANTIFIERS:**
  Overgeneralized words

  Examples: *all, every, always, never, nobody*

  *"**Every** thought you have can assist you in going deeper."*

- **MODAL OPERATORS:**
  Words that indicate lack of choice

  Examples: *should, must, have to, can't, won't*

  Impossibility: *"And your conscious mind **can't** even imagine all the good things in store for you."*

  Necessity: *"And when you discover what you **must** do to relax."*

- **PRESUPPOSITIONS:**
  Statements in which one part is not questioned.
  - **Subordinate clauses of time:** *before, after, during, as, since, prior, when, while*

*"Do you want to sit here peacefully **while** we discuss this?"*

- **Ordinal Numerals:**
First, second, another

  *"You may wonder which insight will come to you **first**?"*

- **Or**
Presupposes which one, not if.

  "I wonder if your new behavior will appear today or in a week's time."

- **Awareness Predicates:**
Know, aware, realize, notice.

  *"Do you **realize** how much you have already integrated?"*

- **Adverbs and Adjectives:**
Presupposes the noun/verb

  *"How **easily** can you begin to relax?"*

- **Change of Time Verbs and Adverbs:**
Begin, yet, proceed, end, start, stop, continue, already, still

  *"You can **continue** to relax."*

- **Commentary Adjectives/Adverbs:**
Fortunately, luckily, thank goodness, happily

  *"**Fortunately**, you have all the resources you need."*

- **EMBEDDED COMMANDS:**
Embedded directives

  *"You can begin to **relax now**."*

  *"You may, Fred, **look deeply** into this situation."*

- **EMBEDDED QUESTIONS:**
Raising question without allowing an overt response

  *"I'm wondering **what you would like to gain** from this."*

- **NEGATIVE COMMANDS:**
  Stating what you do want by using the word "don't"

  *"**Don't** have too much **fun** with this exercise."*

- **ANALOG MARKING:**
  Setting the directive apart with nonverbal analog behavior
  (pausing, volume, tone, gestures)

- **CONVERSATIONAL POSTULATES:**
  Yes/no questions that elicit a response.

  "Would you like to talk about it?"

- **AMBIGUITY:**
  More than one possible meaning

  - **Phonological:**
    Words that sound alike with a different meaning; words used as verb or nominalization.

    *"I want you to be **here/hear** now what I say."*

  - **Syntactic:**
    Adding "ing" to transitive verb and placing it before a noun.

    *"This is **integrating knowledge** from your unconscious mind."*

  - **Scope:**
    When unclear how much of the sentence an adjective/verb/adverb applies to.

    *"I don't know **how soon you will fully realize** that you are sitting here comfortably, listening to the sound of my voice, and you are learning from your unconscious mind."*

  - **Mumble:**
    Trailing off at the end

    "And I wonder how much you are aware … ?

- **Selectional Restriction:**
  The attribution of qualities to something which by definition could not possess these qualities.

*"The very **walls are satisfied** with your progress."*

- **Quotes:**
Giving responsibility to someone else for the message.

"As my uncle used to say, "Everyone has all the resources they need."

- **Utilization and Incorporation:**
Use any event, or behavior of the client, to deepen the trance.

- **Fractionation:**
In a countdown induction, reversing the counting periodically accomplishes fractionation - deepening trance.

*"Ten ...nine ...eight ...seven ...**eight ...nine ...eight***"*

- **Tag Questions:**
Puts question at the end.

*"You are feeling more comfortable, **aren't you**?"*

- **Linkage:**
Begin with something that is already occurring and connect it to something you want to occur.
  - **Simple Conjunction:** *and*

    *"The office has a certain smell **and** the drill makes a lot of noise **and** you can know that your comfort is a top priority for all of us."*

  - **Implied Causative:** *as, while, during, when*
    *"**As** you listen to the sound of my voice, you can quite naturally begin to go deeper inside ..."*

    *"**While** you are sitting here with the nurse beside you, you can take some deep breaths and begin to relax."*

    *"**When** you call for information on 7-day cruises, you are probably able to imagine how nice it will be."*

    *"**During** the noise of the thunderstorm, there is a certain peace you can feel."*

2. Basic Interventions

Anchoring

An anchor is an aspect of experience (visual, auditory, kinesthetic, olfactory, or gustatory) that brings back the whole fullness of the experience, with the feelings that you had then.

- Listening to old songs (auditory),
- Smelling something from childhood (olfactory),
- Tasting certain foods (gustatory),
- Seeing certain gestures (visual),
- Hearing certain voice tones (auditory) . . .

These are all examples of aspects of experiences that can bring back the feelings (be they positive or negative) of those times.

- **Triggers** are a type of anchor that was unconsciously associated with experiences that were stressful in the past (e.g., parents using certain vocal tones or words when punishing children, perhaps with certain gestures visually). We can be triggered today in situations where other people match visually or auditorily these earlier learned patterns, and we may begin to feel negative states beyond what would be appropriate in the current situation. Phobias are generally another class of this phenomenon.

Keys for Effective Anchoring

1. Intensity and purity of state accessed
2. Timing of anchor (when in doubt, anchor early)
3. Uniqueness of Anchor
4. Accuracy of duplication

ANCHORING EXERCISE

ANCHORING TRIGGERS TO A DESIRED RESPONSE

Triad: (True Friend, partner, assistant)

- True Friend: have your partner demonstrate a behavior they don't like in others, one that causes them to react in a negative or unresourceful way. Have them demonstrate the full posture and voice of the person who triggers them, and have them give a context or situation where that has happened.
- Teach the assistant (third person) to do that behavior, fine-tuning posture, gesture, voice, etc., until the assistant can cause the response you don't like.
- Get them out of the situation–shake it off.
- True Friend asks partner, "What would you like to experience in this situation?" True Friend assists them to identify and access (visual, auditory, kinesthetic) the new response, and anchor it with a touch. **
- The assistant does the behavior again, while therapist holds the resource anchor. (Observe to make sure client maintains the desired state while assistant is doing the behavior.)
- True Friend: Test by directing assistant to do the behavior again (without holding the resource anchor) as you observe your partner's response.
- Future Pace. (Imagine a situation in the future when this same trigger happens, and notice what is different)

* Reminder: Identifying a response is often quite different from accessing a behavior.

You can identify something in an intellectual or detached way. Accessing means fully experiencing the desired condition or response *now*. Anchor only when the person is actually experiencing the desired condition or desired response.

COLLAPSING ANCHORS EXERCISE

INTEGRATING POLARITIES OF MIND

- Sorting the Polarities in left and right hands.
  True Friend: Help your partner to sort out a conflict of two opposing points of view (polarity or dichotomy of mind). Have them hold their hands out to the

sides. Use the left hand for one side of the polarity, and the right for the other. Have them look into the hand as they are speaking, and imagine they can see, hear and feel this part of the mind in that hand. Also, if it isn't naturally discovered in the process, have them discover what the positive function of each part of the mind is.

After both sides of the polarity have had the chance to be explored, the next step is to integrate the two by combining or integrating the anchors for the two sides. One way of accomplishing this is to bring the hands together slowly, having them in trance and with eyes open feel the two parts coming together and integrating. (This process is best supported by the use of appropriate language patterns and supporting nonverbal behavior.)

• Integration of Polarities:
  True Friend guides the partner through the following sequence:

• Mutual appreciation of outcomes: "Now look straight ahead, so you can see both hands. Watch both of the polarities as they turn to face each other. Ask each aspect if it understands the value of the other aspect. Allow each to acknowledge some appreciation for the valuable function of the other polarity."

"Now watch and listen to both of these valuable aspects of mind… and allow your two hands to come together only as fast as those two aspects can blend and integrate in ways most comfortable and useful to you … in such a way that neither aspect loses anything … retaining the usefulness and importance of both … each gaining from the other the qualities and capacities that are lacking in themselves, and present in the other."

• "Now allow your hands to rest somewhere on your body … allowing this integration to happen on every level … and even as this integration can continue to deepen in its own way … and the positive feeling of this harmony can resonate through all time … you can also be aware of the Pure Awareness beyond the duality of mind … unchanging awareness … present before, during and after this process … Take a moment to let go of all mind and form. What if none of this is real? What if all of this is made up? What is real?"

STEERING BACK

Change History

- Identify "Present Condition" and create Anchor #1
  True Friend: Help your partner identify an unwanted feeling or state and have them connect this to a particular memory from their past history.

  "I want you to remember a time in the past when you felt that ... Perhaps noticing what you were seeing and hearing at that time ... "

  When they are associated with the "Present Condition," anchor it.

- Break state: Have them come back to the present moment, letting that memory go. Take the time to ensure the negative feeling is not currently being experienced.

- Test Anchor #1.
  Make sure that firing the anchor causes them to experience the kinesthetic response of the "Present Condition."

- Identify "Desired Condition" and create Anchor #2
  "What would you like to experience in that situation?" "How would you like to respond? ... "(perhaps feeling and responding in a way that is more satisfying and useful).

  "Has there ever been a time when you have experienced this?"

  "What if you allowed yourself to experience that fully right now ... seeing, hearing and feeling what you did at this time?"

  When they are fully associated with the "Desired Condition," anchor it.

- Getting a Strong Anchor:
  It is essential that your partner has a strong and effective anchor to the Desired Condition. You can repeat the above process as needed, using other past experiences, or using "What if" to have them imagine being someone else who experiences the Desired Condition even more fully.

  Transferring the Desired Condition to the past memory associated with the original undesired state:

"Take this ... (fire anchor #2 and keep holding it) back to that problem memory (fire anchor #1) and find out what happens as you relive that old experience in a new way. Take all the time you need and let me know when you're finished." (Take both anchors off: the resource of the Desired Condition has been transferred to the unwanted experience.)

Time for integration:

When this transfer has fully integrated … ask a question, get them to talk.

Test Integration

"Think about the problem memory."

Or, fire anchor #1.

Notice the results of the History Change. If you have been successful you will find that firing the anchor to the original problem state (Present Condition) will now elicit the desired response.

STEERING FORWARD

Future pace

"Now I would like you to think about the next time you might encounter one of these situations in the future (fire anchor #2) knowing that you have this resource fully available to you."

Future Pace again, but this time without firing any anchors.

Ally From the Future

This is a very useful process for releasing early childhood trauma, and for experiencing unconditional love. Rather than going back and reliving the trauma, in this process we are going back as an "Ally from the Future" to rescue the little child from the traumatic experience. First we are going to nourish the child with unconditional love. Imagining a golden cord connecting heart to heart, fully loving and accepting this young child just as he or she is. The child does not have to change, does not have to be good, does not have to be pretty or smart, the child does not have to do anything … just be loved as he or she is. And then in this love, you can teach this child whatever she may need to learn and give her everything she needs to deal with this trauma differently.

There is no need to re-experience the trauma. If you are identified with the trauma you can't be the Ally. So before you go back in time to the little child, you need to establish in present time all of the resources you need.

You may find it easy to remember a time that you want to go back to. But if you cannot remember a particularly traumatic time, you can Anchor the symptoms that show up as the Present State, and in trance, trace those symptoms back to discover, "How did it start?" You may uncover memories you did not even know were there. Very often, memories of trauma are blocked out from conscious awareness, but they are still running subconsciously and creating conditions in present time.

When you go back in time to the memory from which the child needs to be rescued, first you are going to see the scene dissociated and learn anything you need to learn from it before you change it. Find out what is really going on. This is very important. Once the lesson is learned, then you go back and rescue the child, and give her what she needs, love her, feel the connection. You don't want to change the memory until the lesson is learned.

You may find that in abuse cases, there is a very complex emotional situation going on. Often the child feels guilty and somehow responsible, and if there is any pleasure involved he or she may feel ashamed. So the possibility of this exercise is that you can go back to these memories and learn whatever you may need to, and then bring all the love and resources the little child needs, to heal this experience and finish it.

You want the Ally to have whatever is needed, like love. I used "Ally from the Future" with a woman whom I asked, "Did you ever love?" And all she could come up with was that she loved her puppy. So I used her puppy as an anchor. I said "I am going to bring the puppy in now, can you feel the love?" I anchored the love she feels for the puppy and let her take that back to the child. A lot of self-loathing may show up in people's memories of their childhood. So you want to establish that the love is there first, and then anchor it. "Is it possible to love this younger child?" And then give the little child everything.

When you are four or five years old and things are happening, you don't know that you are going to make it. You don't know that you are going to live through it and your life is going to work out okay. Just bringing that good news back helps to diffuse an enormous amount of tension and fear, which can finally be subconsciously released.

In the most profound work that you are going to do, you can trace the symptom of the Present State back … perhaps to when you were nine … to when you were six … to when you were three … and maybe all the way back into the womb. It is as if there is a whole string which gets cut. It is especially crucial to defuse particular memories around three to five years old, when the character fixation crystallizes, as well as memories of the birth process.

ALLY FROM THE FUTURE: OUTLINE OF THE PROCESS

1. Find Submodalities of Present State, create anchor #1. (You can use this anchor to trace the present conditions back to an earlier time.)

2. Find Submodalities of Desired State, create anchor #2. Be sure to access and anchor all the resources (love, trust, courage etc..) the Ally needs to bring back to the child. You may want to briefly preview the memory if what is needed is not clear.

3. In trance, go back as an Ally to a time in your childhood when you experienced some trauma or difficulty. Use the anchor #1 to trace back to the appropriate memory. Remain dissociated from the memory, able to view it comfortably.

4. First watch the memory dissociate and discover the lesson you need to learn before you change this memory.

5. Enter the scene as an Ally from the Future, and make contact with the little child while firing anchor #2, bringing him this gift. Give your younger self unconditional love … perhaps while holding or rocking her, and looking into her eyes … See and feel a golden cord connecting the heart of the Ally with the little child's heart. Notice the physiological change in the child. Give the younger self all the resources she needs.

6. When the child is fully experiencing the love and the resourceful state, switch positions, and associate fully with your younger self. Become the child held in the loving attention and support of the Ally, and allow some time to fully have this experience of being in a young body and having an Ally, and all the resources you need in this memory.

7. Next, again associate with the Ally and invite an even older and wiser enlightened Self from the future to appear. Receive a gift from the wiser and older Self. Exchange gifts with the child. Allow both to dissolve in your heart.

8. Future Pace to a similar circumstance in the near future.

Soul Connection

Here is a process of completing unfinished business in relationships, which can be an appropriate aid to someone when they are ready to release the identification with "their" side of the story and are willing to experience the underlying good intentions of both perspectives. This process is designed to go directly and simply to the recognition underlying their differences, that both souls want happiness for themselves and the "other."

This can allow for a sense of "completion" with the suffering involved in wanting others to change. It can also be an opportunity to deepen a soul connection, and to meet in the truth of One's Self.

1. Enter Rapport. This usually involves eliciting the Present State.
2. Establish Desired State. If the client is ready and willing to be finished with the "suffering" that is presently associated with the "relationship," then this may be an appropriate process to use. But it is important to first establish that this is what they want and are committed to. This is a key.
3. Create appropriate Anchors.
4. Pace and Lead the client into Trance. Lead client to a place where the process can safely and comfortably happen. You might want to use the following shamanic metaphor of "meeting at the top of the world."
    You can have the client imagine they can leave their body (as a cloud, dissociated awareness, etc.) and float up to the top of the world, seeing the place your bodies are located getting farther, and farther away. You can use visual, kinesthetic, and auditory suggestions to deepen this trance.
    You may want to establish an easy yes or no signal, such as a "nod" or a "finger raise" in order to be able to effectively track the client's progress:

"And by nodding your head, you can let me know when you have done that."

At the outer edge of the earth's atmosphere, the client can pass through a membrane which, once crossed, allows you to meet with any soul from the past, present or future.

Once at the top of the world, have the client meet an ally to be a guide, who can bring you to the person you want to meet, and be a supportive presence. The ally may be someone dead or alive.

5. Fire the Anchor. Have the guide bring them to the person they wish to meet, and begin the following process:

6. While remaining sensitive to the client's state and how they respond to what you say, ask the client the following questions. You may want to ask the client to let you know with a nod, when they are ready to move on to the next step.) Be flexible with your leads, as these questions may need to be adjusted to meet the client appropriately.

   - What do you really need to say to them (or show them)? You can take a minute or two to do that right now (usually, but not necessarily, done internally).
   - What do they really need to say to you?
   - What is their positive intention for you?
   - What is your positive intention for them?
   - What do you want from them?
   - What do they want from you?
   - Would you be willing to help each other?
   - Take a moment to help each other now.
   - If there is anything else you need to communicate to each other to complete your interaction? Take the time to do that now.

7. Pace and reinforce whatever integration has occurred.

8. Reverse the induction. Guide client back to body awareness and full integration of senses.

9. Future Pace to test results.

EXAMPLE: SOUL CONNECTION

Eli: Put your arms out straight like this. Imagine there is a magnet in each of your hands and they are very strong, pulling each other towards each other. It is magical! What happens when they touch?

Client: *My fingers are kind of locked together.*

Eli: Yes. They are locked together? Infused. Like a solid mass. No way of separating. Totally infused together. You can try. It gets … very good. Very good. So in a moment I will touch your hand and you can drop down even deeper … now … Now! Very good. And down even deeper. And down even deeper. It's very good.

Now in a slightly different way if you were to imagine yourself falling down backwards and down. That's right. Your eyes are blinking – and they can shut.

And as your eyes relax you can imagine yourself falling down into a very safe and easy place of trance. That's very good.

And as you are falling down it can be a cloud or a feather. I am curious as you are falling if you can start to see a number. And I don't know what number it is you are seeing.

Client: *It's a 3.*

Eli: Very good. Let this number have a special healing color. A color that is deeply meaningful for you! And as you watch this number and this color you find yourself relaxing down even deeper. And as this number slowly starts sinking in the horizon, you find yourself sinking down even deeper into a deep trance. And each number that appears will be a signal to your conscious mind to drop down even deeper.

And let the number 4 appear right now. Very good. And this number 4 can be in a different color. A very peaceful color. I don't know what it would be like. But you can let this peaceful color of that number 4 spread through your whole body.

And on top of your head it starts melting. Let this color melt down through your whole body. Bringing a deep feeling of peace. Let your whole body float in a deep feeling of peace, inside and outside. And this peace starts permeating every cell of your body, the veins, capillaries, so nourishing. A deep sense of peace. That's very good. Very good. And now as this number 4 starts sinking in the horizon what would it be like? That's right and down even deeper. And it is good to know that you can always do any adjustments so that your body is comfortable. And you can even forget about the body and drop down. You can always come up and down even deeper. That's very good. As this number 4 slowly fades into the distance–it becomes so small that you can't even see it. And you fade back to an even deeper peaceful resting. That's very good.

And now the number 5 can mysteriously appear way out in the distance. You can see it in a very beautiful color. And as it gets closer and larger and closer and larger you discover yourself so interested in it that your conscious mind drops down even deeper. That's very good. And this number 5 can be even bigger than you are. You can even sit on it. Can you imagine sitting on it? Very good!

And the number 5 is like a leaf, falling down, deeper and deeper to a very peaceful comfortable place. That's very good. Very good. It can feel so good to finally let go. Everything can drop down. In a special way. Because you are so creative, you have such a great imagination. You have your own special way to drop down even deeper. That's very good. Very good. And so now, what we are going to do. It's time to really finish. And to finish this business.

And to finish this business what I want you to do is to imagine that you have a cloud around you. Packed around your toes. You are fully supported by this cloud. And it is going to lift you out of your body. I'd like you to imagine that you look down on your body from above. When you can do that, let me know. And down even deeper. It is very good. Very good. So what are you experiencing now?

Client: *I don't know how to do it.*

Eli: That's right. You don't know how to do it. So what if this part of your body that doesn't know how to do it can feel like a vast space. Can you imagine that? Very good. Now this ball of energy in this vast space can start to float upward, higher and higher upward, and you can imagine yourself sinking down.

You can always come up and drop down even deeper. That's very good. And down even deeper. Now what I am going to ask you to do since the body is now comfortable and relaxed. Let the body park in automatic. Draw all the awareness away from the body and turn it into a very deep place. As if you are falling away from the body, into a very deep safe center in the body. That's it. Are you aware of that now? Good. Very good. That's right.

So your body will take care of itself. And your awareness can be like a bubble of emptiness. In the very core. And this bubble of awareness can start to float up. And you can imagine what it feels like to float up and look down. Can you do that now? Very good. And you will float up even higher. Since you have this cloud to protect you, you can float up even higher. And as you float up, you can see this house and yourself even more deeply. You can see the whole island of Maui from above. And now you can continue to float higher and higher. And now you are going to turn away from the earth.

And you go up higher and higher up until you get to the upper world. And when you get to the very top, let me know. When you get to a barrier. Now you are going to pass through that barrier. And when you do that let me know by nodding your head. Very good.

And so now what we are going to do is we will ask the soul of your father to come here and finish this once and for all. And for that we will need to find a messenger. I don't know what this messenger will look like. When you find it, let me know.

Now ask the messenger to find the soul of your father to come to the meeting. Will the messenger do that?

So when your father shows up, let me know by nodding your head. Very good. So now I am going to take this left hand. And with the other hand you will look at him. Very good. That's right. And now from this position let him know what it is that you need to tell him now. And when I release the hand, peace is going to deepen.

You let him know what you need to tell him. When you told him, you let me know by nodding your head.

Now ask him what he needs to tell you to finish it.

When he has told you what you need to know, let me know by nodding your head. Very good. And so now what I would like you to do, is for your father to tell you what his positive intention towards you is.

When he has told you, let me know.

Pause. Very good.

Now let him know your positive intention towards him.

And so now why don't you ask him what he needs from you in his present circumstances. What does he need from you? And let him know what do you need from him? Now can you both agree to help each other. So help each other now. Yes. Yes.

And if there is anything left for both of you to finish, you can finish it now.

When you are both complete, let me know.

Very good. So now you both have realized that you have chosen each other to play roles in each other's dramas. He chose you and you chose him in your drama, in his drama. And now this movie is over. And there is nothing left.

What happened if you both opened your heart, being completely open-hearted towards each other?

So is there anything else that you need?

Client: *No.*

Eli: Very good. Yes. Very good.

So you can slowly come back from there. Drifting down. Going back to this barrier. Going back to the earth. You can see Maui below you. You can even see yourself seeing you. Feel yourself in your body.

When you are ready, your eyes can open.

Client: *(Laughs, cries)*

Eli: Gratitude can be so beautiful!

Discover the Lesson from a Painful Memory Session with Alexis

Eli: So what is this memory?

Client: *Being with my mother when she found her child in a pond dead. I felt like I was experiencing the death of my only child. In fact, it was a gift, but it was also traumatic.*

Eli: So there is still some obvious charge with this. What would you rather have?

Client: *I don't know.*

Eli: What is really important for you to learn from this before you try to make it go away or change it in any way? What's the key? There is something very valuable!

Client: *It's not happening now.*

Eli: That's true. It is not happening now. What if this memory is a teaching story? You have carried this teaching story for so long, it may have a very important lesson for you, I don't know what it is, but would you be interested to find out?

Client: *Yes!*

Eli: Good. So here is what I would like you to do, if you could just put your hand as lightly as possible on mine … just as lightly as humanly possible, really lightly. That's it, really light, very good. So this hand only goes down as slowly as you find yourself sinking down, even deeper. That's right. You might be interested to discover that the hand can be actually held up by a cord. It doesn't need any effort on your part, just like it is floating there, just as if it was detached, there is some energy around it. You can perhaps feel that energy right now, and it's as if the hand were floating of its own accord, but that part of you that has held on to this memory for so long wants you to learn something. I don't know what it is, but as the hand, that's right, the part of you that knows the lesson is now controlling the hand. So the hand can now be controlled by the deeper part of you that knows the lesson of this memory and so what I would like you to do, is we are going to make the memory into a movie that you are going to see at a distance. So you are going to see yourself in the movie. As you are watching this movie from beginning to end, you are going to be sitting here, and this hand is going to direct you to notice something you hadn't noticed before in that memory. Something very important to learn.

And so what you can do, in a moment I am going to touch you on your left knee, and when I do I am going to ask you to start running that memory as if it were a movie on the wall behind me, and you are going to look at it, and learn from it. I am going to touch you on your left knee, and you can start running the memory now! That's very good. Very good.

When you know what the important lesson is of this memory you can let me know by nodding your head. Yes. Yes. This learning is going to go very deep. It's going to integrate and something will release deep inside from this recognition. Very good. Yes. Very good. Did you learn it? (she is visibly moved).

Good. So now what we are going to do, is when I touch your knee again I'm going to ask you to close your eyes, and this time you are going to relive the memory, only this time you are going to enter the scene, you are going to go to the younger self, and you are going to teach her what it is that you have learned, so that she will learn it too. So when I touch your knee your eyes can close, and you are going to relive this memory again, only this time you are going to go to the younger self and teach her the lesson. And when you are finished, you let me know by opening your eyes. Very good. Very good.

So what a gift. Yes. So now that hand is only going to come down as slowly as that gift integrates in at a deeper level, so that there is an integration. And as that integration happens the very quality of the memory changes, perhaps the colors change, maybe the sounds change, but there is a deeper integration as the lesson deepens in you. Yes, so the hand slowly, slowly starts coming down. As the integration of the lesson starts moving all the way through time, because that lesson starts connecting events all the way back to childhood and all the way into the present moment. Suddenly there is an integration and an understanding of something that has had deep, deep importance.

So even when you were a little girl, this was a lesson you were searching for, and this integrates. And as the memory changes, and the lesson integrates and deepens, it washes all the way through, back to when you were just a little girl. And an understanding happens, it changes the tone of everything. That's right, the hand is slowly going deeper, as the deepening happens on all levels. That's good, very good. Yes. And this deepening of understanding is going to change your relationship with your children, your relationship to your moment to moment life. All is going to shift effortlessly, now that this recognition has deepened. Very good. Very good.

Your hand is close to touching, which means the integration is all the way through; from the furthest past into the present, it will affect everything. And your finger is going to touch, and the hand relaxes, very good, connected.

Would you mind telling us what you learned?

Client: *It was something about the avoidance of life. Always pushing these experiences away. And what I did at the time was I pushed her away, I pushed everything about it away. For years I couldn't even look at my mother.*

Eli: How beautiful. So now if you think of that memory is there a different quality to it?

Client: *It feels soft.*

Eli: Beautiful. Everything is going to change. The pushing away becomes an embrace.

Explanation

This is really a big part of your job as a therapist: to confirm. To confirm that it is as it is.

If you have kept the memory this long, and it still has a deep, profound, emotional charge for you, learn the lesson before you discard it. And what you will find is that if you do not learn the lesson, it will not work. There is an ecology to the system that will keep the memory recurring until the lesson is learned.

If you stick your hand in the fire and you get burned, well, that's a good learning. But if you remove that learning, you will stick your hand in the fire again. But once you have learned it, and you know not to stick your hand in the fire, then you don't need the trauma of the original burn. The lesson has been learned; it's been integrated. You don't have to be traumatized every time you think of fire, you've got it, you are not going to do that anymore. So then you can let it go.

In every moment there is an inherent teaching and an inherent lesson. And if you get it, then you don't need to carry it around as baggage. But if you have been carrying it around as baggage for twenty years, learn the lesson of it so you can then let it go.

Originally when I was doing the hand catalepsy with her, I gave the suggestion that the hand was going to drop down as she dropped into trance, and then something shifted, so I gave the hand a new meaning: the hand is now going to be associated with the wisdom of holding on to this memory in order for her to learn something. So now the hand is a signal to drop into the trance induction for finding the wisdom that's underneath the suffering. And now this hand becomes the anchor for this deeper wisdom that is going to help her learn and integrate the lesson.

What are you going to find if your client is in a collapsed, negative emotional state? How are they going to do the work that needs to be done? Because they have already so bought into the movie that they are not going to be experiencing the resources they need to have in order to do the work.

Student: *Is there a time to let them cathart for a while?*

Eli: Sure, if they haven't yet. And she did.

I minimize it because the catharsis is a way of releasing the energy. Rather than release the energy, keep it in the system, and let it be used for change.

If you have never had any cathartic release it can definitely be valuable. But the tendency is to use that as a way of defusing the situation. If it doesn't make it go away, then the next time it comes up you feel you have to cathart again. But you can use this energy. Rather than crying it out or hitting a pillow with it, use it to make the change that is needed.

Now we are dissociating from the picture. Using the submodalities, we put the picture farther away. And by putting the picture farther away, suddenly she is not as emotionally identified with it. Now that she is not emotionally identified with it, she can start to look at it with fresh eyes and learn the lesson.

It is very useful to have the flexibility of having someone move into a memory or move out of a memory. Having them associate or dissociate. Sometimes it is very important to have them associate into the memory, so that they can fully experience what has been avoided. Sometimes it is important to dissociate to have the space to see it more objectively.

If you are Empty, then inherently you will recognize the natural ecology of the situation!

Discussion after the Session with Alexis

You lead her a lot, that was very different than from the way we have been working. You said you will notice, everything is going to change, you seemed to be more directive than when I have seen you work before.

And yet in the direction, it was content-free. And so it's really giving Alexis confirmation. That is really a big part of your job as a therapist. To confirm. To confirm that it is as it is.

When we worked with Alexis earlier and asked her if she wanted to change the memory, she said she wanted to leave it as it was.

Yes, beautiful. You see if there is something to learn, you don't want to throw away the learning. If you have kept the memory this long, and it still has a deep, profound, emotional charge for you, learn the lesson before you discard it. And what you will find is that if you do not learn the lesson it will not work. There is an ecology to the system that will keep the memory recurring until the lesson is learned. If you stick your hand in the fire and you get burned, well, that's a good learning. But if you remove that learning, you will stick your hand in the fire again. But once you have learned it, and you know not to stick your hand in the fire, then you don't need the trauma of the original burn. The lesson has been learned, it's been integrated. You don't have to be traumatized every time you think of fire, you've got it, you are not going to do that any more. So then you can let it go.

In every moment there is an inherent teaching and an inherent lesson. And if you get it, then you don't need to carry it around as baggage. But if you have been carrying it around as baggage for twenty years, learn the lesson of it so you can then let it go.

If you are staying Empty, then inherently, you will recognize the natural ecology of the situation.

Phobia Cure Process

1. **Deliver two standard reframes**

   "Most people learn to be phobic in a single situation that was actually dangerous or seemed very dangerous at the time. The fact that you were able to do what is called "One-trial learning" is proof that your brain can really learn fast. That ability to learn fast will also make it easy for you to learn a new response."

   "The part of you that has been protecting you all these years by making you phobic is an important and valuable part, and we want to preserve its ability to protect you by updating its information."

2. **Minimally Access Present State (Phobic state)**

   "What happens when you become phobic?"
   "How do you know you have a phobia?"

   You only want to elicit enough of the phobic state so that you have a reference point. Be aware of the behavioral shifts (breathing, posture, facial expression, color, etc.) that occur when the phobic state is accessed, and use this information later when testing, in order to know when the state has been changed. As soon as you can see that the person is accessing the phobic state, interrupt by breaking state in whatever way is necessary.

3. **Create a strong Anchor to the Desired State (safety and comfort):**

   "Think of a time in the past when you felt very safe." (hold anchor)
   "Think of another time when you felt really comfortable and safe." (hold anchor)

"Think of someone else who can feel this even more deeply ... what if you could have the experience ... of seeing through their eyes ... hearing through their ears ... and feeling as deeply comfortable and safe as they can feel ..." (hold anchor)

You can help the client to relax and enjoy the process by pretending that you are going to watch a movie together. Most people have pleasant associations with going to the movies. A good way to set up the anchor is to hold hands while you are eliciting the desired state ... *"And you can squeeze my hand when you feel it really strongly"* ... (and you squeeze back). When you watch the movie together you can have them give your hand a squeeze whenever they feel any discomfort, and you can squeeze back–firing the anchor.

4. **Establish 3-place dissociation**
   a) *"With your eyes open, imagine that you are sitting in the middle of a movie theater, and you see a still black and white snapshot of yourself on the movie screen. Let me know when you have done that."*
   b) *"Now float out of your body up to the projection booth."* (With a phobia of heights, dissociate to a seat in the back of the theater) *"You can see yourself sitting in the seat in the theater, and also see the still black and white snapshot on the movie screen."*

You can have them indicate to you where in the room they are imagining their "double" is sitting, and where the screen is. You can use hand gestures to keep the three places cleanly sorted, and look at the "screen" with them when they are running the movie.

5. **Run black and white movie–First have them give the movie a name:**
   "Watch and listen to a black and white movie of yourself in one of those situations where you have had this phobia." (Have them watch the worst time, the first time, or a recent time.)
   "I want you to watch the whole event starting before the beginning of that incident to after the end of it, when everything felt okay again. Watch and listen as the younger you goes through that experience, while you simply watch as a detached observer, as if it had happened to someone else. When you are done with that movie, stop it as a still picture, and let me know."

If the person had difficulty doing this, then:

- Chunk down the stimulus, so that the person sees, for instance, only every third second of the movie, or only the bottom half of the movie at the first showing.
- Use additional submodalities to increase the dissociation: see the movie farther away, smaller, fuzzy, etc.
- Utilize the kinesthetic system. "Put your hands on the plexiglass and feel the cool hard surface that separates you from the movie."

6. Run the movie backwards

"Next I want you to leave the projection booth and step back into yourself sitting in the audience, then step into the still picture at the end of the movie, and run the movie of that experience backwards in color and very fast … all the way back to before the beginning of the unpleasantness. Okay, go ahead."

7. Dissociate again, Run the Movie a second time–discover the Lesson

"This time while you watch the movie … I would like you to become aware of something that you might need to learn from this … so that you can release this phobia completely …"

Repeat step #6 again … running it backwards in the same way.

8. Run the Movie a third time and add a Soundtrack

"So if this movie had a soundtrack, what would it be?"

"So this time imagine you could hear this soundtrack as the movie runs all the way to the end."

Repeat step #6 again … running it backwards in the same way.

9. Testing and future pace

Attempt to re-access the phobic state in any way you can.

"What if you were in that situation now?"

"Imagine being in one of those situations right here."

Observe nonverbal response and compare what you see with the earlier response (#2). What had been a stimulus for the phobia state should now no longer be significant. If you still get a phobic response, check that the person followed the procedure exactly.

"What was it like when you did that?"

The person may have added or subtracted steps. If they still have only a portion of the phobic response, have them repeat the procedure exactly, but faster each time, until none of the phobic response remains.

10. Reassociate and bring out of trance

11. Closing

"Since you have stayed far away from those particular situations in which you used to be phobic, you may not have had the opportunity to learn about them. As you begin to encounter and explore these situations in the future, I want to urge you to exercise a certain degree of caution until you learn about them thoroughly."

Example of Phobia Cure: Molly

USING HAND-SQUEEZING FOR ANCHOR

Eli: Classic phobia is one-time learning. The organism is so smart that once it has come close to death or experienced danger it will never expose itself to that experience again. Every time a person thinks of the dangerous situation, the anxiety recurs. A person will have an anxiety attack and decide never to go into that dangerous situation again. Was there a first time when this happened?

Client: *It was when I was a little girl and stole a peach from a fruit stand. I was about four years old. I ran away and dropped the peach and I've never been able to touch a peach since. I get nervous talking about it.*

Eli: You can let go of that for now. Just stay present here. Leave the other out there. We're going to make believe we are watching a movie and before we do, I'd like you to get into a space of absolute comfort and relaxation. Do you enjoy going to the movies? We're going to watch the movie out there. Let's get into a useful position. I would like you to sit side by side with me.

I want you to get safe, comfortable and relaxed and the more you feel that, I'd like you to squeeze my hand and I'll squeeze yours back. (Anchor #1)

Good. Has there ever been a time when you've been even more safe, comfortable and relaxed than that? Can you imagine yourself being in that moment? That time when you were totally safe, comfortable and relaxed. Allow yourself to feel that in your body. Let the sensations get even stronger and squeeze my hand to let me know that you are feeling that. Even stronger, through your whole body. (Anchor #2)

Maybe there's another time in your life when you felt it even more strongly—more comfort and relaxation. *Good.* I'd like you to go to that time now, looking out through those eyes, seeing what you saw then, feeling that feeling. You can hear what you heard then, making it even stronger. *Very good. Very good.*

Are there any other times when you felt really safe, comfortable, and relaxed? Do you have another one? Looking out through those eyes, hearing any sounds from that time, feeling those feelings, letting them get stronger, feeling it deep in your body. *Very good.* When you are ready, you can come back.

(First Run of the Movie)

Now what we are going to do is watch a movie projected on the screen over there. I don't know what the title of the movie is, but it is about a little girl stealing peaches.

Here's what we're going to do. You watch the movie only as long as you feel comfortable, safe, and relaxed with me. In order to do that, you might want to make the movie black and white. We're going to go as slowly as you need to in order to watch if comfortably far away. If at any point you start to feel uncomfortable, you stop the movie and come back here.

When the movie gets to the end, when the little girl has thrown the peach away, or at the end, you're going to run it backwards from the end. Everything is going to run from the end to the beginning.

Also, I'd like you to imagine that you are going to float up and out of this chair and into a projection booth, where you are going to have the controls for the movie. The Molly in the projection booth is going to be able to look down and see the Molly down here. The Molly in the projection booth can run the movie more slowly, can stop it, can turn it off if it starts to get uncomfortable and, when it gets to the end, start to run it backwards.

Client: *It really is uncomfortable now!*

Eli: Then let's stop it and come back to here. Let's forget about that and just stay present with me. What do you need to feel more comfortable?

Client: *I've got a big judge in there.*

Eli: What does the judge say?

Client: *You shouldn't have taken that peach!*

Eli: I'm curious, would the judge like you to learn the lesson of the peach?

Client: *Yes.*

Eli: *Good.* So would the judge support you in learning your lesson so completely and thoroughly that you can let go of the suffering?

Client: *Well, I'm thinking now that the judge didn't get satisfied because I used to steal things after that and then I stopped, totally. I wouldn't think of taking anything.*

Eli: He wasn't satisfied because you kept stealing and now he's like an electric cattle prod, kind of sticking it to you, making sure you learned your lesson.

Client: *I never thought of it that way.*

Eli: So, I appreciate the judge wanting you to be honest and you appreciate the judge. You actually learned the lesson of honesty. Is the judge willing to try to experiment to find out if Molly will keep the lesson of honesty without the suffering?

Here's what I'd like from the judge: If it turns out that Molly didn't learn the lesson of honesty without the suffering and she starts stealing again, I would like the judge to bring back the phobia of the peach to teach her. Would the judge be willing to do that?

Client: *Sure. No problem.*

Eli: Okay. So, now we are going to watch this movie. Do you feel comfortable now?

(Eli fires Anchor)

Does this bring back the comfort and security? *Very good.* Now I'd like that part of you to float up into the projection booth and we're going to watch this movie. What will the title of this movie be?

Client: *Girl Steals Peach.*

Eli: Okay, *good.* Now let's start this movie in black and white, but I want you to put a musical soundtrack to it. What kind of musical soundtrack could you put to this?

Client: *Fiddler on the Roof!*

Eli: "Fiddler on the Roof." *Good.* Now, I want you to hear the music and we'll start it rolling. See the credits, its "Girl Steals Peach" starring Molly. Then I want you to watch it as slowly as you need to stay comfortable and present here with me–watching it on the screen. When it gets all the way to the end, run it backwards, listening to the music. Did you run it backwards? What happens when you run it backwards?

Client: *Peach goes back. Little girl goes backwards.*

Eli: Okay. That was our first run. How was that for you?

Client: *Good!*
(Second Run of the Movie)

Eli: Now, what we are going to do is add color and let the music get a little more lively, because it is kind of becoming a bigger production. " Girl Steals Peach" starring Molly. And we'll float up into the projection booth where you have the controls. If at any point you start to lose this comfort, you can stop the movie, but now run it through again, and when you get to the end, run it backwards. *Good.* That's run two.

Now, what I want you to notice here, as the movie runs, it automatically runs backwards and then we break state. We stop and we talk, because what you don't want to do is set up a continuous tape loop. You don't want it to run forward and backwards and forwards and backwards. What you want to do is to run forward, backward and *stop.* Forward, backwards and *stop!* So what you are doing is actually repatterning the memory cells so that it runs forwards, backwards and *stop,* but running backwards is a way of deconditioning it. It actually seems a little absurd, funny. The peach suddenly goes back to the cart, the girl backs away.

Client: *I actually was looking at the other fruits on the cart.*

Eli: It changes the quality. It depotentiates it so the charge is starting to be dissipated.

(Third Time)

Now we're going to do it a third time, only this time, at the point where the girl is running away and she has dropped the peach, I would like you to enter the scene. Go to her. Thank her for going through that suffering so that you got to learn a very important lesson. Let her know what the lesson was and let her know that she, having learned the lesson, can start to forgive and let go. Go up into the projection booth, now watching. *Good.* How was that?

(Fourth Time)

Now we're going to do it one more time, but rather than being disassociated into the projection booth, I'd like you to bring that part of you back into your body and we're going to do it without the anchors and just run it on your own as fast or as slow as you want, in full color if you want, and just watch it go and then run it backwards.

Great! How was it?

Client: *Good! I got to tell the judge I learned my lesson.*

Eli: *Good!* That is the ecology check. The ecology check is "Molly learned her lesson." Once she has learned her lesson, the suffering can go.

That's wonderful! Is there anything left you need to communicate to that little girl?

Client: *Yes, that she's a good girl.*

Eli: Let her know that. Tell her. Did she get it? We know you're a good girl now.

Client: *I wasn't a totally bad person.*

Wrap up:

Eli: And now, when you think about peaches, there's a difference.

Client: *I was amazed at how nervous I was getting before just talking about peaches!*

Eli: Yes, and peaches can be so juicy and sweet and now that you've learned your lesson and you are a really good person, you've proved that to the judge over the years. Now you can have them back. If you start stealing again, the judge will take them away from you. Can you imagine yourself having a really juicy peach with the skin on? (Future pace.)

Client: *Just about.*

Eli: You may want to start by peeling skin off and having just the juicy part.

Client: *I've had people peel them for me.*

Eli: But you can peel them now.

Client: *Yes, I can.*

Eli: I don't know where we can get a peach for you to try.

Follow-Up

A week later Molly's husband, having heard about the session came to the retreat bringing a big sack of peaches. Molly reported that the first bite was "Orgasmic!"

Example of Phobia Cure:
Post-Traumatic Stress Disorder

As you sink down … and down even deeper
There can be all kinds of feelings inside.
But as your mind and body settle down,
your eyes are blinking, because they want to close.
They can get heavy – and you can keep them open
As long as you feel comfortable.
You can close them whenever it feels comfortable.
It doesn't matter. *That's right.*
And down even deeper.

And as you fall in to a safe, comfortable place–
I don't know what that place would be like for you–
But you know that there is a very, very safe and comfortable place,
where nothing can touch you, nothing can harm you.
And when you can find a place like that inside yourself
you can let me know by nodding your head. *Very good.*

Now, what I am going to ask you is: you are going to stay in this place,
and we will go to a movie theatre together and we are going to watch a movie of your
trauma from this place of safety. *That's right.*

And when the body reacts and the emotions react
but you can stay in a place of safety and watch this movie.
All from a distance, where it doesn't touch you,

it doesn't hurt you.
So we will be in a movie theatre together
In this place of safety, with your eyes open.
So stay exactly where you are.
Let your eyes open now. Let's open them. *That's right.*

Let's look out there and as we are going to watch you can hold my hand if you like– as
a place of anchoring–a place of safety.
I like you to watch the movie with the trauma and when it gets to the end I want you
to watch it roll backwards. *That's right.*
Staying safe right here.

And when it goes all the way to the end, watch it go backwards.
And when it goes all the way back, let me know. *Very good.*
Now I'd like you to add a soundtrack of music,
as you are watching it.
And let it go all the way to the end and when it goes to the end
have it roll back all the way to the beginning with the music
and let it go to the start and let me know when it's over. *Very good.*

Now there is something very important for you to learn,
that's why you have been holding on to it.
When you have learned what you need to learn from this,
let it sink in and let me know by nodding your head!

What is there to learn? *Very good.*
Now that you have learnt it, it doesn't need to be like this anymore.
So now you are going to watch the movie with the soundtrack
only there is going to be a difference.
There is going to be an intervention by an outside force: by you!
You will come in as an outside ally and change the movie.

So watch the movie now, start with the music,
and when it gets to the crucial moment, you will enter the movie
and you are going to change it.
When you have done that successfully

and it goes all the way to the end,
let it roll back to the beginning and let me know
by nodding your head. *Very good. That's really good.*

And so now, this time, you are going to enter the movie as the victim,
but not playing the victim anymore. You are going to act freely.

And you are going to do it in a completely different way.
So now enter the movie–doing it completely differently.
Watch it till the end and then rewind it and let me know.
Very good.

And now we can take everything you have learned from this.
You can close your eyes and take it into the very place
that still feels wounded and bring this in as a healing balm.
Go into the wound that's still there somewhere
And bring the nectar of this–
your capacity to not be a victim–
to change it–to having learned from it,
and notice how that healing can sooth the wound. *That's very good!*

And I am going to let go of your hand
And you have the full capacity inside yourself now. *Yes. Yes.*
What's your experience?

So now if you remember that horror …
Can you remember it with new eyes?

Yeah! (laughing)

Yes. Beautiful. Thank you!

Nesting of Emotions and the Black Hole

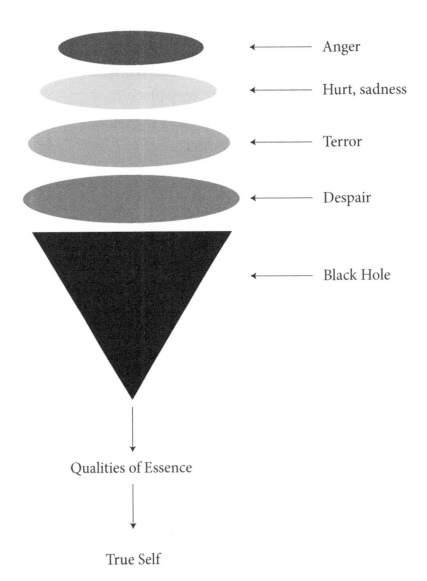

Anger

Hurt, sadness

Terror

Despair

Black Hole

Qualities of Essence

True Self

Emotions are limited. They have a beginning, a middle, and an end. Generally, when feeling a negative emotion, there is a sense of it being endless, so we stay above them.

We try to suppress them, avoid them, resist them and distract from them. We tell a story about it as a way to disassociate from them.

Most people live in superficial emotions and create a story about themselves or others or the world, as a way to avoid the deeper emotion. To bring awareness to these levels of emotions can bring a clarity and profound insight into what is really going on at a deeper level.

If you are willing to plunge into any emotion; if you are willing to say, "Okay, it is a good day to die, come and get me," and then dive in, you can discover that underneath each emotion is another emotion. And under that emotion is another one. If you are willing to go all the way, eventually you will come to despair, and under the despair is the black hole.

The black hole is the way home, beyond all thoughts, all ideas, all form. It is the doorway to emptiness and Being. Under the black hole, you discover the truth of your Self. You discover essence.

This particular illustration of the Nesting Pattern of Emotions is true for most people, but not all. You will find that some people are wired differently.

The Enneagram, which we will be examining in detail later in the book, provides a map for the different character fixations and how their emotions are nested. For Nines, the most surface emotion is not anger, it is sadness. Under sadness there is usually fear. It is much easier for a Nine to feel sadness and fear than it is to feel anger.

For a Nine to get in to anger, it is very close to despair, very close to the explosion of hopelessness. This is also true for certain self-preservation Sixes, because for the Six to feel anger could be dangerous for survival. Many Sixes who mistake themselves for nines, say, "I don't get angry, I am helpful." Helpfulness is a way of staying safe. Anger becomes suppressed and is closer to despair.

You will also find that it is possible to drop from anger directly into essence. It is possible to drop from sadness and hurt directly into essence. Or from fear into essence.

What usually happens, is that if you drop from fear or sadness directly into essence, you have skipped a couple of steps. You have skipped despair, and you have skipped the black hole. These will now be waiting as latent tendencies. This will then have to show up at some point to be experienced.

There is no problem with this. You can fall directly from anger into bliss. Then if you stay in bliss long enough, expect sadness and fear and despair to show up.

They will. The tendency then is to say, "I lost bliss, something is wrong with me, I lost it." You didn't lose it. Bliss did not go anywhere, sadness and despair have shown up in bliss to be burned, to be thrown on the funeral pyre. If you don't touch it, if you don't identify with it, it will be burned.

The key is not to act on it and not to suppress it. This is really the revolutionary news. Because, basically, all our lives, we have been taught to either act it out or suppress it. Either it is not appropriate to feel this, or, "I shouldn't feel this so I will make believe it's not here."

The possibility is, as everything arises, not to move. In order to not move, you can't have a story. If you don't have a story, you will discover you have a quiet mind. And in a quiet mind, you will become very subtly aware of the impulse to fixation. Don't go anywhere. The tendency is to go somewhere. The tendency is to go into the thoughts, to be mentally dissociated into a story about what you should or shouldn't do.

It is simpler than that. You don't do anything. This is the giving up of the character fixation, the surrender of the doer. When you are willing to give up the doer, there is enormous relaxation. It is giving up all effort. When you give up all effort, then whatever arises can be experienced directly. Without judging it, without suppressing it, without acting it out, and without creating a story about it. This is the simplest and easiest. This is the end of suffering inherent as a character fixation, and the beginning of endless revelation as the Truth of Self.

USING THE BLACK HOLE IN A SESSION

The black hole is a profound invitation to the client to meet their emotions directly, and discover the inherent limitedness of it, and what is underneath. It is an invitation through the layers of unmet emotions into essence.

There can be a tendency to jump on the first emotion the client reports and invite them to drop into it and go through the nesting of emotions.

This is appropriate when the client is asking for ego-transcendence, or is particularly stuck on a recurring emotion that is likely covering something else.

However, during the Present Condition, often emotions are an integral part of a pattern, and the client is seeking to change a pattern, so going through the black hole is not appropriate in these circumstances. Sometimes, an emotion is there to teach something, it is appearing to bring something to the light of consciousness, so it can be more skillful to work with it and see what it has to teach the client.

EXERCISE – BLACK HOLE

Take your partner through the nesting of emotions and into the black hole.

Get into triads, with one person as the True Friend, the other as the client, and the other as the observer.

The True Friend asks the client to elicit an emotion, perhaps something felt recently (not a major trauma).

The True Friend invites the client to open to the emotion, and drop down inside it, to feel it fully and see if they drop all the way in, is there something underneath.

Then when the deeper emotion is discovered, they are invited to drop into that, and fall all the way in, and underneath.

This continues until the client discovers despair or the black hole or goes deeper into silence, or peace or love, etc.

Then swap partners and repeat.

List of Exercises

1. Toward, Away, and Against
2. "Excellent"–exercise
3. Pacing (mirroring) exact words
4. Matching Language Modalities
5. First trance/second trance: pleasant experience
6. Deep trance game
7. Pacing and leading into trance
8. What Does thinking mean?
9. What Does Anger mean? (or sadness, fear, etc.)
10. Submodalities of a Positive/Negative Memory
11. Discovering the Present Condition
12. Discovering the Desired Condition
13. Nesting of Desires to Essential Desire
14. Re-Anchoring Triggers to a Desired Response
15. Collapsing Anchors: Integrating Polarities of Mind
16. Change History
17. Ally from the Future
18. Soul Connection
19. Phobia Cure
20. Black Hole

PART FOUR

Demonstration Sessions

Eliciting Present State *and* Desired State Session *with* Julia

I'm curious, what do you want?

I want to let go of all preconceived notions of how it should be.

Very good, you want to let go of all preconceived notions of how it should be. So, when do you want to do that?

Now.

Right now? Is this the only time?

Always, in the future.

Okay, when is a time when preconceived notions come up?

(the smaller the chunk you can get, the easier it is going to be to get your change, it's that simple. So now she wants to let go of all preconceived notions all the time, she is talking about waking up, but what we are demonstrating is working with a specific change piece.)

When specifically are these preconceived notions a problem or issue?

When I am judging a situation.

Very good, when you are judging a situation. So when have you judged a situation recently?

I feel like I am always judging, but you want a specific time.

Are you judging right now?

When I first came.

Very good, so when you first came you were judging the situation. Very good, so now you are going to teach me how to do that.

Okay.

Okay? What happens?

I definitely had an inner dialogue going on.

So there is inner dialogue. Where do I hear it?

Everywhere, I mean, it's just a very loud voice.

A very loud voice, what's it saying?

How does he think he is going to do this class without handing us anything? (laughter)

Very good. So how does he think he is going to do this class without handing us anything. So where do I hear it? Do I hear it everywhere in my head?

It's just going by.

Going by this way?

Yes, I guess so.

Good. So as this is going by, what is the voice tone?

Yes, it has a tone like you just made.

Good. (He mimics a judging, critical voice again). Okay, what's the speed of that?

It's kind of a normal voice.

A normal voice. Is it your voice?

Yes, but with a little more maliciousness to it. It's kind of like "I know it all."

"How is he going to teach us this class without giving us handouts?" (Eli mimics the inner voice.) So while that is going on what is happening in your physiology? As you say that, I notice your eyes squint down a little bit.

Yes, because I am not trusting, then I might start picking at my fingernails.

Okay, so you are picking at your fingernails, your eyes are squinting, what else is happening physically?

I am not comfortable.

You are not comfortable. So how does that express itself in your body?

I may have had my arms crossed or something.

Like this. (He imitates voice and posture … laughter)

That's good.

What's going on emotionally?

I am not relaxed. I am not feeling comfortable inside.

Yes, not relaxed or comfortable, so what is the emotional state?

Not feeling peace or comfort inside.

So how would I experience that discomfort, I want to feel this also. Is there pressure anywhere? Is there tension?

I would say there is a little bit of tension, yeah. I usually keep it in my shoulders.

Okay, so some tension in my shoulders. What's happening over here?

More closed.

Closed. Okay.

My shoulders are slung.

My shoulders are slung, this is closed, okay. (Laughter) What now?

More dialogue. "I better not give my money until I am sure this is the right class."

(Laughter)

All right. So all this is happening, now what would the desired state be?

The desired state would be to come in and just be very open. And not judging, just feeling, sensing what's going on, and also just trusting that if this is where I am at this time, I am where I was meant to be.

Okay, so teach me how to do that. What's going on physically, mentally, and emotionally?

Nothing really. Your head is quiet, silent. Your posture is up and straight. You breathe fully and deeply, and just relax, be very relaxed.

And then you said I am supposed to have some trust, what would that be like?

The trust is the relaxation.

Okay, good. How will I know when I can trust the relaxation?

There is calmness and quiet.

Okay, so there is calmness and quiet. What about the emotions. Is there anything going on emotionally?

Just a good feeling.

So how do I make that good feeling? Is there a temperature with it?

Warm.

Where is the warm?

In my heart.

So there is warm in your heart. Okay, so is there any emotion?

No, I don't think so, just warmth in the heart.

So warmth in the heart, a quiet mind, relaxed body, open, clear ... good. So this is the desired state.

Yes.

So now if you were to walk into the room like this on the first day, now what's the experience.

Peace and harmony.

Is that what you want?

Yes!

Good.

But, I don't know, can you always be open and trusting when there are maniacs out there?

Well, it depends what you are trusting? Not if you are trusting the maniacs. Not if you are trusting your mind. So this is the question I asked you before. How do I know what the trust is? What do I trust?

I want to say my inner voice, but I don't want the voice to be there.

Okay, good, so you want to say your inner voice, but you don't want that to be there. So what else is there? What else can you trust?

A gut feeling.

A gut feeling. Very good. So can you trust the gut feeling?

In the past it seems that I have always been wrong.

So maybe you don't want to trust the gut feeling. (Laughter.) What else is there? What is more trustworthy than that? What is more trustworthy than an inner voice, more trustworthy than a gut feeling?

I guess just time, time to see.

So are you going to trust time?

I don't like that response either. I really don't know, this is one of my issues.

Very good. So right now if you were to drop inside into a place of deep quiet, can feel your heart warm and open, I am talking about dropping into a place behind your heart. And if you drop in there with the question, "What is trustworthy? What is it that is fully trustworthy? "

My guidance.

143

Your guidance, very good. You can trust your guidance. This is the missing piece isn't it?

Yes.

Fantastic. Yes, so now how do I trust my guidance?

By dropping in.

By dropping in. Very good. So how do I drop in?

Really just by quieting my mind and dropping in.

Yes, quieting my mind and dropping in. Very good, so this is the desired state. Thank you very much.

Demonstration of Trance Induction with Anchoring
Session with Chris

Are you comfortable?

Yes.

Good. Is there any way you could be even more comfortable?

This is okay.

This is okay. All right. So have you gone into trance before?

I imagine so.

You imagine so, yes, that's it. Do you have a good imagination?

Yes.

What I would like you to do, is if you could put your right hand as lightly as humanly possible on mine. That's very good. That's it, as lightly as possible. Very good. So as I am speaking to you … You may discover … that's right … the light has maybe changed … your breathing may be changed … you are swallowing … and all of this … can take you down even deeper … very good, that's right … and what are you aware of now?

The body is starting to settle in a bit. It feels nice.

Yes, that's right, your body is starting to settle in bit, it feels nice. And your head can nod, and as you are aware of looking into my eyes perhaps your breathing is also settling … that's it … and that is a signal that you are dropping down even deeper.

Your eyes are starting to blink … and that may be a signal that they are getting a little tired and would like to close … that's it … and you can keep them open or closed now … very good … and your eyes can relax … you can relax the muscles and nerves of your eyes … so deeply and so completely that they can feel like they are glued shut … You can be so successful in relaxing your eyes Chris, that they wouldn't work even if you wanted them to … because you have relaxed them so much they can feel like they are glued shut. And you can test them now to discover how successful you are … that's it … very good … You can stop testing now and drop down even deeper … very good … very good.

Now Chris if one is completely awake … and ten is completely asleep … you are somewhere in between. And I don't know what that number is, but some part of you knows. One is completely awake, ten is completely asleep … Let me know what number.

Three or four.

Three or four, very good. So I am curious if you can see the number three in front of you. Very good. Now the number three can be a certain color, Chris. And that color can be a very healing color … and it can start vibrating and sending waves of relaxation through your entire body, allowing you to drop down … even deeper … that's very good … Now Chris, as that number three starts slowly sinking beneath the horizon … you find yourself dropping down to the next layer of trance. That's very good … very good … And so maybe the number four can appear … and the number four can be a different color … a very soothing, pleasing color … Yes, that's right. And that color is also vibrating and it is sending out rays … rays that enter your body from the top of your head … massaging your body all the way down through your facial muscles and neck and shoulders … all the way through your chest and arms … your waist, hips, legs … between your toes … That's very good … and as the number four starts sinking beneath the horizon … you find yourself dropping down to the next layer of trance. That's very good, Chris.

Now this hand that is floating there is going to be connected and used by a deeper part of you. And this deep part of you has something very important for you to learn. That hand only goes down Chris … as the other hand starts to lift … and the other hand may feel like there is a helium balloon tied to the wrist pulling it up. And it starts to lightly … lift as this hand goes down … and I don't know which finger … or maybe the palm or thumb or the whole hand will start lifting … slowly lifting … and as this hand goes up the other hand goes down … that's it …

It's starting … the middle … the whole hand slowly coming up … that's it … as if there is a helium balloon attached to the wrist pulling it up gently … very good … the left hand is lifting … the right hand is sinking … and the conscious mind which may be very interested in this process can relax and drop down even deeper … that's very good … the conscious mind which has worked so hard for so long … can begin to let go … to dissolve

… to sink into a very deep … yes, that's it … one hand is lifting … lifting … and the other hand is sinking … sinking … that's right, that's very good, you are doing very well.

Now there may be some time in your past … a deeply traumatic time … when if you had the understanding and the emotional maturity you have now, you could have dealt with that time very, very differently … and I do not know what that time would be … but when you find the right time you could let me know by nodding your head … a time … with more emotional maturity and understanding … you would have been very different in that situation … very good … you know what that time is, but we are going to put it aside for a minute, and we are going to come back to that in just a second …

What I am going to ask you to do Chris … is to remember a time when you actually felt all of the resources that you would have needed to have dealt with that situation differently … and when you can actually feel that in your body you can let me know by nodding your head … very good, and I am going to touch your left knee and those feelings can get even stronger … very good … now being right here, right now Chris … that's right one hand is continuing to go up … and one is continuing to go down … and you are right here right now … and I would like you to even more strongly feel the resources you would have needed to deal with that situation … feel it more strongly … I am going to touch your knee … you can let it get even stronger … now … that's very good, very good … that's it … that's wonderful.

Now the right hand is about to touch, and when it touches Chris … the old memory, the negative memory, the one that you wanted to work with is going to start to appear … the right hand is going down … and as it goes down … that memory gets stronger … that's it … down … memory is coming in color … that's it … you are in that memory now … hearing what you heard … seeing what you saw … experiencing it … and now bring in this (Eli fires anchor) and allow yourself to live it differently … that's very good, very good … very important to learn this lesson … yes … that's very good … very good … Okay … so … so this other hand can slowly go down as your eyes open and you come back … good … and you can drift back down … as the lesson integrates and deepens … and reverberates through your entire life … and you find that as this reverberation continues to happen … yes.. your eyes can open …

Is there anything you need? How was that for you?

The memory came easily and clearly. It was a memory I have worked with before so it wasn't really strong, but I learned something different with it, it was really nice.

Discussion after the session with Chris

In these videos you have watched a lot of people do this arm catalepsy where the arm rises up. The secret that I have found is, you tell the person initially to put their hand as lightly as humanly possible on yours, this sets it up. If their hand is too heavy, you tell them "as lightly as humanly possible." In putting their hand as lightly as humanly possible on yours, they are setting up their own arm catalepsy. Because their arm can't be leaning or resting on yours, it has to be up here. This is the joke–they have made their own arm catalepsy.

Then you make the suggestion that this hand only comes down as the other hand rises up. You are creating a cause and effect: one hand goes down and this causes the other hand to go up. You might have them imagine a helium balloon around this hand to help lift it up. And then you pace it: "I notice the middle finger raised up first … now the palm … "so you are always noticing what is going on and feeding it back to the client. This gives the client permission to continue, gives you some authority as a therapist that you know what is happening, and allows the process to go along smoothly.

Why are we doing that with the arms?

The reason you are doing that is that you are engaging a deeper level than the conscious mind in this process. It's like Chris said earlier, his mind came in and went to the hand and said, "It's okay, there is something going on here." It's a reality check that there is something going on beyond the conscious mind just making it up. Because there is some other kind of response that the mind is not involved in, yet the body is responding. It deepens the trance and sets up an anchor to a "deeper level of knowing," which is now going to be helping in the learning process.

Examining the Nesting of Emotions, and Dropping through the Black Hole. Session with Jordan

As everything falls away as the days go by, it feels very uncomfortable.

What specifically is falling away?

It feels that the momentum of my life is stopping, my doingness, just having the invitation to stop. It's so overwhelming for me.

Yes, so when the discomfort comes up, then what happens?

Well, it feels very uncomfortable, because it feels like there is nowhere to run.

Okay, so, "It feels like there is nowhere to run" is actually a thought, it is not a feeling. So this is very good–now we are starting to make distinctions between thoughts, feelings, and behavior. So the thought is, "there is nowhere to run." And that thought itself is a dissociation from the feeling.

Well, it's fear.

Fear, very good. So right now if you were to drop into the fear directly, without the thought, just dive into the fear for a moment … and let me know what is even deeper. What is it the fear is hiding? There is something even deeper under the fear, a deeper feeling.

It's immediately more comfortable just with the invitation to dive into it.

Good. So what's underneath it?

Feeling lost.

Very good. So now just close your eyes and drop into the direct experience of feeling lost. Let yourself experience it directly. And sink into it as if there is nothing else left except feeling lost. And as you sink in, it's as if there is a weight attached to your consciousness that pulls it in completely. So wherever you look it's feeling lost, whatever you feel is feeling lost. And as you sink into that, even deeper, what's underneath feeling lost?

Kind of a desperation.

Very good. Desperation. So now drop into the desperation. Let yourself feel the desperation completely, without any separation, without any thought, just sinking into the complete desperation … hopeless, helpless, there is nowhere to go, no help. And as you sink all the way in, it's as if there is a weight on your consciousness pulling you down to the very middle of this desperation. So it's inside, it's outside, it's everywhere. No separation. Just desperation. And then discover what's even deeper. What's underneath desperation?

I feel like I am falling backwards.

Yes, that's it. Very good. But rather than being in the body, stay in the emotions, and just allow yourself to fall now. This is what's been avoided, this falling. So let yourself fall all the way into it. Completely into it. Into this vast, black, dead emptiness. Just falling in. And when you get all the way to the bottom of it, let me know what is at the bottom.

A little pin-prick of light.

Yes, so just allow yourself to keep falling. Falling all the way through.

It's very dense.

Yes, that's right, so now fall into the denseness. And how would you describe the denseness, where are you?

It's all consuming.

Yes.

Imploding.

Yes. Good, so implode completely as you continue falling. Let me know what is at the bottom of that. What's after the implosion?

It's quiet.

That's right, it's quiet. Let yourself sink completely into this quiet. And let me know what is the quality that you find there?

It's very beautiful.

Very beautiful. Very good, very good. So let yourself sink even deeper into this deeper quiet. Discover if there are any limits to it. How deep can you go into this beautiful quiet? Keep sinking into it. Find out, does it get even better as you go into it? And what is your experience?

It just goes on and on.

Yes, it just goes on and on. So now as you continue sinking in, let your eyes open.

Yes, that's it! This is what has been avoided. So you never need to come out. You can keep sinking further and further and further into this beautiful quiet. Eyes open, eyes closed, doesn't matter. And then the momentum of your life continues as it does anyway. But you don't have to be involved. You don't have to worry, you don't have to struggle, you don't have to do it. Because your interest is how deep is this beautiful quiet? Is there anything even deeper? Is there anything even more beautiful? How deep can you go into it? And then you fall in love with it. And then when you fall in love with it you find everything that you had been looking for in the other direction. So that becomes the consuming passion of your life–how deep into this beautiful quiet can you rest?

Thank you so much. Now you are radiating beautiful quiet.

Finding the Crystallization of Fixation
and
Dropping through. Eli tells a story to Deepen the Understanding.
Session with Lara

What do you want?

Peace, quiet.

Yes, peace, quiet. So what do you have instead?

Peace and quiet only sometimes, and in between grabs of a pattern coming.

What is this old pattern coming that grabs?

One of the patterns is the fear of doing something wrong. Fear is the old pattern that comes out of the blue and grabs the whole body. I would like to not be a victim of this fear. It happens when I drive by the restaurant where I work.

So it happens when you are driving by the restaurant, when does it start?

I was almost to work and one of the people I work with was driving behind me, and WHAM, I was totally unprepared, and it just hit me like that. That showed me that day that there is still something there that is not clean.

What's there that's not clean?

The whole minestrone of worthlessness, failure, fear, unlovable, left alone, you name it, it is a big pot of soup. So you put everything you can think of in the pot and it's boiling on a low flame, and then something turns it up and (makes a sound effect of increased intensity). So I would like to disconnect the flame, to get rid of the flame.

Fantastic. So I am curious, when you saw your partner and looked in the rear view mirror, what was the next thing that happened?

I felt pain, something grabbed me here and there was a knotting. There was a feeling of failure and a loss of love. That is mostly what was in the pot, and it was spiced up with unworthiness and all these other things.

Failure and loss of love, spiced with unworthiness. Like a big minestrone.

So my life seems to be so nice now, but somebody keeps turning up the heat. So then I know the soup is still there. So even though I can pretend that I have freed myself 99%, that 1% seems to be what is keeping me from cooking the real thing.

So what have you done to let go of the other 99%?

I listen to Gangaji a lot. Then I went through the physical pain of letting go of what I loved, and what was a part of my creation, and what I totally identified with. But I haven't let go of it yet. I haven't let go of my need to be reflected through others. I am not totally comfortable with the way I am here, a nobody. So I am trying to create little niches again, and that in itself is a hook. I am still not free to just be. It has something to do with looking outside to others and being identified with what I do.

It's so beautiful, so clear, you have done really good work. In your willingness to see, and in your willingness to tell the truth to yourself, you have done so much, as you say, 99%. That's fantastic. You see the identification and you notice the suffering it causes. And you notice that in the identification there has to be a creation so that someone will give you back the reflection. That's fantastic. And now what you are asking for is to finally take away the burner, take away the soup, the sense of worthlessness.

I really don't know who I am without anything. There are spaces where there is nothing and it is great, but they don't last very long.

What happens?

The endless engine starts.

Are you ready to unplug that engine?

Yes, I would like to.

Have you ever done trance work before?

Twice before.

(discussion about past trance experience)

So that symbolic game at the restaurant started much earlier. So what we are going to do together is to go back to the very roots of where that whole game started, and what choice was made and how that can be done differently.

Okay.

So what I would like you to do put your hand as lightly as humanly possible on mine. Yes, that's it ... just as lightly as humanly possible ... That's very good. Now I know that you have gone into trance before ... and you can allow yourself to have permission to go in at least as deep this time ... Good ... Very good ... As lightly as possible ... And you can discover the depths are so deep and you can relax ... and drop down ... and something inside ... relaxing and allowing you ... yes ... to find something, a slight sensation ... very familiar ... maybe from the past trance work, and maybe just before you go to sleep at night ... I don't know what it is like for you when you finally finish the day ... and you finally have to stop thinking about anything else ... if you keep thinking you will never go to sleep ... you turn towards the pillow or feel yourself comfortable ... and let yourself go ... drifting ... and letting go of everything ... and dropping down ... even deeper ... that's very good ... very good.

And this hand only goes down as slowly as you go down into a very deep, profound trance ... that's right. Now in a moment Lara ... I am going to touch your forehead ... and when I do you may feel a slight sensation of some sort ... When I touch your forehead your eyes will close and you will drop down ... into an even deeper profound state of trance ... You are doing very well, very well ... You may notice how the light has changed ... how the images have changed ... and all of that is a signal that your body has changed ... with slight involuntary motions ... as your consciousness sleeps. What you call waking is sleeping ... and what you call sleeping is waking ... as the deep part of you ... the part of you that has been guiding you ... that part is awake as the conscious mind finally rests and sleeps ...

And I am going to touch your forehead ... and when I do your eyes will close and you will drop down much deeper ... I am going to touch your forehead now ... very good ... very good and now Lara I am going to say "One, two, three, open your eyes" and when I do your eyes will open as you drop even deeper in trance ... And when I touch your forehead your eyes will close and you can drop down even deeper ... "One, two, three open your eyes" ... good ... and deeper (touches forehead). One, two, three, open your eyes ... good ... and deeper (touches forehead) ... very good ...

and the hand is slowly going down deeper and deeper and deeper … and when your hand touches Lara you will find it's like something opens inside and you … down … now … that's it … the conscious mind deeply resting … sleep … and as your hand touches that is a signal to drop to the next level … very good …

Now, Lara what we are going to do … I want you to imagine … that we are in a tall building that has the same amount of floors as your birthday … now I don't know how old you are … but that is how many floors this building has … what we are going to do is take an elevator … down … to the very correct floor where this whole minestrone started … and so I wonder if you can imagine us standing … waiting for the elevator … and then the light comes on and the little tone that lets us know the elevator is here … that's it … and the door is open … and now we are going to get in the elevator together … and that hand will slowly come up and push just the correct floor … that hand slowly, slowly … that's it … and you are going to push … and let me know what button it is we are pushing …

Four.

Four … very good … so now we are going down … all the way down … from the thirties … and perhaps you can even feel your body as this elevator drops to the twenty-ninth floor … twenty-eighth … twenty-seventh … and perhaps you can see those numbers flashing in front of you … each number taking you back … down … twentieth floor … nineteenth floor … eighteenth floor … seventeenth floor … each number flashing … dropping you down deeper … and deeper until we get to the fourth floor … and when we get to the fourth floor, Lara … and the door is open you are going to see a scene … and this scene … when you were four years old may be familiar or may be unfamiliar … and you are going to start to see something that is very important … to discover something … how this whole minestrone got started … let me know when we get to the fourth floor, before the door is open … so we are still in the elevator … when we get to the fourth floor … before the door is open let me know …

We are there.

Okay, can you see the number four flashing?

Yes.

Very good … So in a moment the door is going to open … and when it does you are going to step back into being four years old … let the doors open and step in now … and let me know … what do you see?

I see a garden.

You see a garden. Very good. So start walking in the garden … I don't know if you can smell the flowers in the garden … let the colors in that garden get really bright and clear … and what would it be like to feel your feet walking through this garden … and see those little four-year-old shoes … what kind of shoes are they anyway?

They are two-year-old shoes.

They are two-year-old shoes, very good … very good … and now what is happening in this garden? Who else is here with you?

I am by myself.

You are by yourself. Very good. And what are you experiencing?

It is nice. Very nice.

Very nice … Good … Is this garden related to the place where you grew up when you were two years old? … So what if it were time to go back inside the house?

It's no fun inside.

That's right, it's no fun inside. So let's go back and discover how come it is no fun inside …

It's dark and boring and nobody to play with.

Dark and boring and nobody to play with, very good … Was there anyone taking care of you when you were two years old?

My mom's around.

Your mom's around. Where is she?

In the upstairs.

Yes, in the upstairs. Let's go visit her … that's right it's not fun at all. Let's go … it's very important. Is she in her room?

In her bedroom.

Very good so let's go into the bedroom … And what's happening?

I don't really feel like it.

You don't really feel like it. Tell me … why don't you really feel like it? What are those feelings?

She is not going to play with me anyways.

She is not going to play with you anyways. How is she going to treat you?

Okay.. There is just nothing there, you know.

Yes, just nothing there. Very good. So now let's discover if there really is something there … that this little two-year-old girl hasn't noticed yet … You know it may seem like there is nothing there and she doesn't want to play … but sometimes there is something even deeper that two-year-old eyes don't yet see. Would you be willing to discover that?

Okay.

So let's go knock on her door and see if she lets you in.

The door is open.

The door is open. Very good. Is there anything you need to say as you come in? When you look at her, what do you see?

She is pretty.

She is pretty. What else?

She is unhappy.

She is unhappy, very good … so why don't you ask her, why are you unhappy … yes …and what does she say?

She doesn't say anything.

She doesn't say anything … So now look in her eyes … look in her eyes … because even though you are only two years old, you have some deep secret wisdom … something you have learned over so many years … that is still with you even though you are two years old … look in her eyes and what do you see?

She looks as bored as I am.

Very good. Maybe that is where you learned it. Is that where you learned how to be bored?

Well, there is nobody to play with.

There is nobody to play with … is that where you learned that you need somebody to play with in order to be happy? … very good … where did you learn it? You are doing really well … very well … that's very good … so let's leave this bored mother and go back into the garden.

That's better.

Let me know when we are there?

We are already there, we flew down the stairs. We flew down the stairs! I can still fly.

You can still fly, very good. Now that we are in the garden what do you want to do?

Just hang out.

Just hang out, okay … well, I have an idea … what if there was some special friend in this garden with you?

There are none.

Just you alone?

It's not bad.

Not bad. Would you like to learn something? A secret? It's a secret about boredom …

Okay.

So when we went into mom's room it was dark and boring, and when we went out in the garden it's not so boring … right? What is the difference?

Well, the house is all grownups. And the garden is okay because there are trees, and you can peel off the skin … but it makes an owie when you peel them …

So wouldn't you like to feel as good as you do when you are in the garden even when you are in that big grownup house? That would be good, wouldn't it?

Yes …

So is there a way that you can feel as good as you do in the garden, even in the grown-up house? Or even better? How would you find a way?

Don't know.

Don't know … very good, but you would like to find out … Yes, very good. So here is the secret. Is there a garden inside of you? … How would it be possible to find the garden inside of you? So what I would like you to do is to start to look inside. When you first look inside you may first find boredom, can you find boredom?

When you said there was a garden, there was a garden.

Very good, when you look inside you find a garden. Now what I would like you to do, is to look inside and find boredom … It's very different from finding a garden, because there are no pictures, are there? What is there instead?

Dark brown wall.

Very good. A dark brown wall, so the picture of a dark brown wall has a certain feeling. Can you feel it? What that dark brown wall feels like?

Like fake velvet.

So let yourself feel that.

Uckk.

Yes, it's an ucky feeling … and you have been running away from feeling it … But in order to learn the secret we have to go through it … so let yourself feel it … it will get better … but first you have to feel it … Can you feel it?

Yes.

So now, since you are flying so well, what if you could just fly all the way through it … even deeper underneath it … flying down into it … what's underneath it?

Flying down to the bottom, then there is pain.

Yes, that is it! You are finding the secret … Now little girls don't like pain, and you have done everything you can not to feel it … you hit the boredom, and the boredom is better than the pain … but we are finding some magic here … some very important magic that you forgot from so long ago … So would you be willing to go into the pain?

Sure.

So drop into the pain now. Let yourself sink into the pain. That's right, what is even deeper? What is under the pain?

It's white.

It's white, very good. And what is the feeling that goes with the white?

There is no feeling there.

So let yourself drop into the space of no feeling. (She sighs.) That's right and what is under that space of no feeling? Yes, what is that hidden feeling that was hiding way down there? Way out of sight?

It's again the fear of not doing it right.

Very good, the fear of not doing it right. That's it … you are not doing it right. So let yourself feel that.

Now my feet are asleep and I am afraid I am not doing it right.

So you can be comfortable, you can move your body … now feel that feeling of not doing it right … how perfect that you can feel it just now, it all comes together in that moment … feel it fully, and what is even deeper under that feeling?

Some relief.

Yes, so let yourself fly into the relief. And as you are in the relief, I am going to tell you a story … You can listen or not, it doesn't matter … Sometimes little girls like to have stories told … and this is a story about a little girl who lost happiness.

Once upon a time … a long time ago … in a far-away land … there was a little girl who lost happiness … And she didn't know where she lost it … so she became very, very sad … and very anxious … and she thought, "What if I never find happiness again?" And she didn't know what to do …

So first she went to her mother and said … "Mom, I have lost happiness" … but her mother was not interested … she said, "Go outside and play" … So she didn't find happiness there … Then she went to her father and said … "Papa I have lost happiness" … and he said … "Don't worry, you will find it when you grow up" … so she didn't find it there either …

Then the little girl thought, Well, if I am really going to find happiness, I will have to make it up … I will go out by myself and I will make up happiness … I will make myself into a princess with silver slippers … who can fly and have magic … and then I will be happy." So she made believe she was a princess with silver slippers who could fly … Well it wasn't boring … but it wasn't the happiness that she was looking for either …

And then she thought … "I know … I don't have happiness because I don't have friends … so I will get some friends … But since I have never had friends … I don't know what to do to get them … so I will make myself so pretty … that then my friends will come and they will want to be with me …

So she went into her mother's closet … and she found a costume … and she found her mother's make-up … and she made herself really pretty so that her friends would come … And sure enough, they came … friends came … and she tried to act so perfectly … that her friends would like her, and then she would find happiness … but that didn't work either … It was fun … it wasn't boring … but it still was not the happiness she was looking for …

So then she thought, "Well, if I have a boyfriend then I will find happiness" … so she decided to grow up really quickly … and she made herself just right to have a boyfriend … And then she thought … "This will bring happiness … but how do you act with a boyfriend?" … she had never had one before … so she didn't know what to do? And so she decided to become the perfect thing that would make him happy … and then she would find happiness … And since she was such a smart little girl … and since she had worked so hard to do it right … she made herself into the perfect little girl … that every little boy would love … and she got a boyfriend … And it wasn't boring … and sometimes it was fun … but it wasn't really the happiness she wanted …

Then she thought … "I need to be bigger … if I have a woman's body … then I will have happiness … because then I will have a man and be happy " … So she grew herself really fast into having a very beautiful woman's body … and became very, very attractive to all the men … And it was fun … but still it didn't find her happiness …

So then she thought … "I am going to have some children … that will make me happy" … and so she had a little girl, and that made her very, very happy …

It wasn't boring … but it still was not the happiness she was looking for … So then she had a little boy … and that made her happy for a while too … but it was not the happiness she was looking for …

So by now she kind of gave up on finding happiness … she forgot that it was even a possibility … so really what she wanted was to be artistic and creative … so she found a career … and she became very artistic and very creative … And it wasn't boring … and sometimes it was fun … and by now … she had even forgotten about happiness …

And pretty soon she became an old lady … and there was a certain sadness … and she didn't know where it came from … and a certain bitterness … and she didn't like the taste … And she didn't know where that came from either … She'd had a family … she'd had a career … she'd had a husband … she had everything … why should she be sad? Why should she be bitter? She didn't know … she had forgotten that she was looking for happiness … On her deathbed as she started to die … she made a wish: She said … "If I ever come back, I want to find out really … what is happiness?"

And sure enough she died … and she came back as a little girl … and even in her mother's belly she started worrying … "Am I going to do it right this time? … Am I going to be perfect? … Am I going to do it so right this time … am I going to find happiness?" So she decided that she would be a perfect baby and then she would find happiness … And when she was born she was a perfect little baby, a very pretty little girl … But she didn't seem to make anybody happy … she didn't make her mother happy … she didn't make her father happy … and she couldn't even make herself happy …

So then she got very nervous … "I must not be doing it right … I have got to discover what to do" … And then one day when she was very, very bored … she went out into the garden to play … And in the garden were these beautiful old birch trees … She knew she shouldn't peel their skin because it was an owie for them … but she decided without even knowing why … that she would just hug one of these birch trees … And as she hugged it … something deep inside realized … that all along she had been looking for happiness in all the wrong places … And the birch tree started to teach her … "Dear little girl … under the boredom, under the fear … under the terror that you are not doing it right … there you will find happiness."

And when she heard this news, it was hard to believe … but what to do … As the wind blew it rustled the leaves of the birch tree … and she could hear the leaves talking … They said … "Don't worry … there is nothing to do … you don't have to play any role at all … you just have to be willing to go in the direction of the boredom … the direction of the fear … the direction of the terror that you are not doing it right … because happiness is hidden there."

When she heard this news she recognized that it was true somehow … but she didn't know how it would turn out in her life … And the birch trees rustled and said, "That's right, my dear, you don't know how it will turn out … but you will find happiness no matter how it turns out … So which direction are you going to look?" … the birch tree asked … "towards happiness … or to how it is going to turn out … how you are supposed to act?" And the little girl made a decision … then and there, she decided … no matter what, she was going to find happiness.

Now I don't know how this story relates to you and your garden … or what decision you will make … but I am curious how this is going to resonate … how this is going to relax everything … into the deepest recognition of the truth of where to find happiness … that's very good

… so when you leave here today … you are going to grow up into this imaginary big body … and get into an imaginary car … and when you drive down the street … when you get close to the place where you work … you are going to see a signal that is going to remind you of the birch tree and its story … and you will recognize what a gift … to have little signals planted everywhere you look … that can remind you of the birch tree and its story … that's very good … very good …

So if right now you were to take off all of the disguises … the disguise of a cook … the disguise of being a young girl … the disguise of being a woman … taking off all of the disguises … that's right … What is your experience?

Just space.

Just space, that's right. And if you drop the "just," there is "space" … And we can call that space happiness. So now staying exactly there, let your eyes open … And what is your experience?

Lightness.

Lightness, yes. Lightness and space. Your head can slowly turn and look out into this room … And what is your experience?

Embarrassing. I have never done something like this, it is very beautiful to look into all of your faces. Thank you.

Discussion after the Session with Lara

I wanted Lara to have the direct experience as a little girl alone in her garden of going through this. Two to four was the time frame, and that is when the fixation is crystallized. It is already coming in in the womb, but this is where there is a crystallization of it.

What I wanted was for this little girl in the garden to be willing to notice that, "Oh, yeah, if I am in the dark house I don't like it, whereas if I am out in the garden it's okay. Over there it's boring, over here it's fine." So it's externally referenced, it's noticing a visual stimulus and reacting. And this is what Lara came in with. The visual stimulus of looking through the rearview mirror, and suddenly an experience. The visual stimulus of driving past the place where she works, and she had the experience. So how she feels inside is externally referenced to what's going on outside.

We find that this little girl already has this structure, so I wanted this little two- to four-year-old girl to have the experience of discovering what is inside. Forgetting what's outside, let's go inside. Let's go through the boredom, because boredom is what she has avoided. She doesn't want to go to mom, mom's boring. She doesn't want to go in the house, that's boring. Let's have fun, let's play, let's make believe, let's fly, let's have magic shoes. Whatever it is.

So the little girl then discovers she can go in. The little girl discovers she can go into the boredom, into this terror, into this pain, into this not knowing what to do, and find that there is some deeper peace underneath it. So now the little girl has learned this. Now that she has learned it, let's now tell the story. So that now the story becomes a reinforcing of what has been experienced, contextualizing it, putting it into a larger frame of past lives, and recognizing the opportunity of this life. So the experience of the little girl going through the boredom becomes the anchor through which the experience can resonate out into the life.

When do you not take them through the nesting of emotions as a way of being okay in life? They may not be ready perhaps, but isn't that ultimately what they have to experience?

Ultimately, yes. Ultimately you have to dive into your Self. And in diving into your Self you will find what's there. This is called inquiry and discrimination. So you dive in and you find anger, "Is that who I am? No!" so then you go through the anger. You find fear, "Is that who I am? No!" so you go through the fear … it's the willingness to keep going in, and discarding what changes, and finding what is always present. If anger comes and goes then it can't be me, because I am here when anger isn't. Okay, fear is here sometimes, sometimes it is not here, therefore I can't be the fear. Keep inquiring to find out what doesn't change. This is the process of self-inquiry, of waking up. Yes, ultimately that is where everybody is headed, but maybe not in this lifetime.

I have worked with clients for a long time, and some people immediately caught what is going on, and with others we never even approached it. They were still working on the more surface ego-strengthening kind of stuff. So that is why we are doing this training, so you can work with people in a full range. You can work with people where they are, not insisting that they go to where you are or where you think they should be.

I realized lately that just seeing people where they are at right now has been very valuable just to allow.

How it will manifest, who knows. This is also a part of the work with Lara. We don't know how it is going to manifest, we don't know how it is going to come out, but however it shows up, happiness is already there. So then who knows what the outside will be. This is really what that session was about. It is switching from the experience that, "The outside makes me happy or the outside makes me bored," to "Happiness is here, and the outside comes and goes." That is really what is possible.

Since she was oriented to the outside, and it came that you told her a story, and the story was about telling her it's okay to go within yourself for the happiness, it seems that you played the part of coming from the outside to offer this message, which was her normal way of receiving things.

You are right that the presupposition here is that the message is coming from the outside. This is why I was very happy when we could have the birch tree telling the story. Because once the birch tree tells it, it is already within the context of her own experience and situation.

Sinking Through the Terror, and Finding Peace. Session with Tom

How do you sink through the terror?

By being willing to experience the terror without running from it or modifying it or trying to make it go away. Without giving it a story of what it means. By cutting off all mental involvement and directly diving into the terror.

The terror is present like a cloak. What I'm hearing you say is, the way to go through it is to go through it, but it gets more solid as I go into it.

Go directly into the solidness of it without having any idea of it, just dive. Go down alone. Sink deeper. Until the terror becomes so overwhelming there is nothing but terror. Call up all your terrors, all your nightmares, let all the terror arise now and face it.

My greatest terror of all is being alone. I can face it but I don't seem to go through it. I've done this about three times in the last hour and it's so physical.

That's because you keep popping out like a cork. Sink deeper like a lead weight. Right now drop into it. What are you experiencing?

It's all closed up, like right now I can't access anything below my throat.

Good. So it's closed up like you can't access anything below your throat. In order to know that you must be able to drop into the very core of that. So not the body and not the mind but directly into the emotional frozen terror that is closed up right in there. What happens when you drop directly into that?

Good, now don't worry about the body and don't worry about the mind just go into the feeling of the terror itself. Pure emotion. And what is even deeper?

Try closing your eyes, maybe that will help you just drop all the way into the terror, so that there is no exit from it. Bigger than the body, bigger than this room, the entire world pure frozen terror and you are sunk right in the middle of it and then like a lead weight you sink all the way through it to the very bottom. Completely alone the entire universe frozen in terror, and what's even deeper when you sink all the way through? What's underneath it?

The ocean.

Good, but don't just see an ocean because that would be mental, just experience it and drop into the ocean, let yourself sink into the very center of this. That's it, sinking in, absolutely, to the very depths of this.

Without moving out of it, without changing anything in your awareness, speak from this and tell me what it is.

Peace

Peace, very good, are there any limits or edges to this peace?

No.

Very good. So let yourself sink even deeper into this peace so it would be like dropping a cube of sugar into this ocean of peace and notice what happens as it dissolves and sinks even deeper, yes. How would you describe your experience now?

I had the experience that I was flowing out.

Is there any edge?

No.

So from here now, where is love?

Everywhere.

Deep peace and love is everywhere. This is what you have been running from, hiding from, yearning for, and your yearning brought you home.

Now the tendency is to pop back up into your head and make this another experience. Keep sinking in … it is endless. Then Peace and Love live this life. Your children will be very happy to discover that Peace is living this life. Everyone will be happy. If you come back up to start living it again, and your experience of Peace becomes "something that once happened," then you are back in the dream. If you stay in and continue to explore this love affair with peace and love, you go deeper and deeper … and it gets more and more subtle … and it gets more and more exquisite ….

Can I learn to take myself down?

Wait a minute, you already assume that you are going. You're already planning on leaving and coming back. Drop all beliefs here. You just discovered that this "me" is not real, that there are no boundaries!

I've never experienced that ever. The terror was total. I've never been able to go through that space before. And here I am.

So that's Grace, you made it through and now it is only your own commitment as to whether you live in this realization or not.

Total commitment.

I am very ready to do that.

Beautiful. So stop planning your round-trip tickets, give up all ideas of any imaginary past or future. Everything will unfold very naturally, very effortlessly.

It feels so effortless, and the chatter is, "It can't be that easy."

Be vigilant, don't give rise to this chatter now. That's a way of putting yourself back to sleep. Chatter is a trance induction. Don't give rise to it, don't go back to sleep. Stay awake.

For many years of your life you have been avoiding the terror, and we spent one afternoon of concentrating on this and you dropped into bliss, into peace. So now you commit your life to it and it just gets better and deeper.

All I want to do is smile.

I know what you mean.

Teaching Stories *and* Inductions

Beach and Waves

Now I want you to imagine yourself on your favorite beach … it may be a familiar beach … or a beach you've never been to before … a beautiful beach, just for you … I am curious … whether there are palm trees growing on your beach … and whether the sand is white and warm and soft under your feet … as you are walking along that beach … And maybe … as you turn around … you can see your footprints in the sand … getting smaller in the distance.

And as you are walking … you can feel the warm sun on your skin … It feels so good … and you can hear the ocean rolling against the shore … and maybe you can even see it … its deep colors … melting with the blue sky … and the air is so fresh and crisp … you can feel the breeze caressing your face … and when you lick your lips … they may even taste salty.

Now I would like you to walk towards the ocean where the sand is wet … there is a wooden stick lying in the sand … I would like you to pick it up and feel it in your hand … its texture … its weight … and now … with that stick, write the number five in the sand … The number five is connected with your body, from your knees to your toes … and as the ocean washes the number five out to sea … your body … from your knees to your toes … goes into … a deep trance.

And you can write the number four in the sand … and the number four is connected to your body from your knees to your hips … and as the ocean washes the number four out to sea … your body … from your knees to your hips … goes … into … deep … trance.

And now write the number three in the sand … The number three is connected to your body from your shoulders to your hips … letting all of your internal organs and your spine relax completely ... all of the nerves and tissues from your shoulders to your hips ... letting go and releasing ... and as a wave comes in ... and the ocean washes the number three out to sea ... and your body ... from your shoulders to your hips ... goes ... into ... deep ... trance.

And now you can write the number two in the sand ... The number two being connected to your body from your shoulders to your fingertips ... and as the ocean washes the number two out to sea ... your body ... from your shoulders to your fingertips ... goes ... into ... deep ... trance.

And now you are writing the number one in the sand ... The number one is connected from your shoulders to the top of your head ... and you can relax all those muscles around your lips ... your eyes ... all the muscles in your forehead ... letting go ... And as the ocean washes the number one out to sea ... your body ... from your shoulders to the top of your head ... goes ... into ... deep ... trance.

And now I am going to ask you to ... walk to another secluded ... safe and private part of the beach ... to draw your last number ... which is a zero ... a zero big enough to lie in ... your magic circle ... you can draw that number now ... and lie down inside ... And as you are lying there ... your mind can deeply relax ... allowing any thought that comes up to sing and dance outside of the circle ... as you are safe on the inside ... quiet ... letting the mind become more and more quiet ... and if a thought should come up on the inside ... that's just a signal ... to relax down ... to let the mind become even more still ... that's very good ... very good ... so even the thought becomes an ally ... as a signal for the mind to relax ... and become even more quiet ...that's very good ... and as your mind is quiet ... your conscious mind can go to sleep ... even as the body is in deep trance ...

So I am curious right now ... if the mind were to become even more quiet ... and as the mind becomes quiet ... if just for a moment ... the body were to dissolve ... and as the mind is quieter and quieter ... and the idea of a body dissolves ... or you can just put the body aside, it doesn't matter ... and you discover yourself floating in deeper ... and deeper ... so that little subtle places of tension start melting ... unnoticed places of holding ... dissolve ... that's very good ... and I am curious ... as you sink in ... to a vast depth ... is there any boundary here? Discover if there is boundary, what is it made of? That's very good ... Is it possible to be aware of infinite space above you? Infinite space in front of you ... vast emptiness to the sides ... vast silent emptiness behind you ... and infinite space below you ... now is there any boundary here? What if the boundaries dissolve now? That's very good … very good …

And now from here … let the thought arise: "I am," and put your name on it … and notice where does it come from? … and what are the effects of this thought … and let it sink back to where it came from …

And now let the thought come, "I want" … let a desire arise … have the thought, "I want …" and fill it in … let it come … notice where it comes from … notice what it is made from … notice the effect … and let it sink back to where it comes from … that's very good …

And now let the thought arise, "What about my past" … let that thought arise … notice where it comes from … notice the effect … and let it sink back … and now let the thought arise, "What about my future" … let this thought arise, "What about my future" … notice the effect … what has to be there … what is underneath this thought, "What about my future?" … and let it sink back to where it came from …

And now let the thought arise, "I need to be recognized" … notice where it comes from … notice its effect … and what is unspoken … who needs to recognize you? … that's very good … very good … and now let it sink back to where it came from … very good …

There is something deeper here … something beyond … what if you were in love with that right now … what would that feel like … where does that come from … what is the effect of being in love with something deeper than this … that's very good … and now without changing anything in your awareness … without moving at all … open your eyes now … and notice … is there any difference between inside and outside … that's very good … and now your eyes can be open or closed, it doesn't really matter … but is it possible … that even as the sense of body consciousness returns … that you don't move … it might seem that your body appears in you … or it might seem that you appear in a body … it doesn't matter … but is it possible right now … that even as body consciousness returns … you don't move … that's very good … very good … and so let body consciousness gradually return … awareness of hands and feet … awareness as if you are in a body … is that possible without moving … the body can move … is it possible that the body can move without you moving … that's very good … taking all the time you need …

Sensory Awareness Induction

You can just sit or lie comfortably and listen very closely to what I am going to be saying to you. I am going to suggest some ways in which you can begin to appreciate your sensory abilities ... in a way that I am sure you will find very interesting ... and there is nothing for you do right now ... you can allow the sound of my voice ... and any suggestions I make ... to allow you to go deeper inside ... and every feeling you experience ... and every image you see ... can be a signal for everything to relax completely ... and you can begin to more deeply realize a familiar peace and stillness ... deep inside ... right where you are now ...

Is it possible for you to become even more relaxed?

(Note changes in breathing, settling in chair, spontaneous eye closure]

If your eyes are not yet closed ... you may want to let them close now ... What if you completely relaxed your eyes ... and relaxed all the muscles around your eyes ... Can you imagine ... the muscles of your forehead ... becoming smoother and smoother? ... and what if this was a signal ... for all the muscles in your face and head to relax ... and let go?

And I wonder how slowly and deeply you can breathe ... can you breathe through your whole body? ... into every cell? ... perhaps you can comfortably hear the sound of your own breathing ... and you may even notice ... that your ribs are expanding slightly with every inhalation?

And with every exhalation ... you may find that your body can become more soft and relaxed ... and you may be very interested to discover ... that you can experience your breathing just like the waves of the ocean ... flowing one after the other ... so easily and comfortably ... and this can be a message to every part of your body that it can relax completely ...

Now what if you were to imagine ... looking at a very beautiful sunset ... can you make the colors even brighter? What if you let the color wash through your whole body ... releasing ... letting go ... ?

Can you be aware of one of your arms feeling heavier than the other? ...

or notice how warm and comfortable your body is becoming? ... you may even be able to feel waves of relaxation ... flowing out of your fingers ... out of your toes ... just like sand pouring out of your fingers ... out of your toes ...

Now what if you saw a beautiful flower a few feet in front of you? … I wonder what color is it? … Can you smell its fragrance? … and allow the color and the fragrance of the beautiful flower … to make you aware of a particular feeling … deep inside …

Perhaps you can imagine the pleasure of relaxing comfortably in a bath of warm water … or how it would feel if you were floating gently and softly on a soft … thick … white cloud …

Can you imagine the sound a brook makes flowing over rocks and stones … around tree roots … I wonder what you imagine that brook would look like … or how it would feel if you were lying near the brook … comfortably in the grass … and you could look up and see … blue sky coming through the leaves and branches of a tree … and you can let this experience be a signal … to allow your mind … to relax … to relax completely … to quietly rest … in a deeper peace … so easily and naturally …

And as your breathing once again becomes like the waves of the ocean … you might even drift down into an even deeper peace … (Wait one minute or so) …

That's very good …

And now can you allow yourself to begin to very slowly … lazily … just drift back to this time and this room … and you can keep all those good feelings of deep relaxation … and you can know now … that you can drop into an even deeper level or relaxation and peace … whenever you want to …

And as you are ready, your eyes can open, even as you remain comfortably aware and relaxed.

And now you can take a deep breath and open your eyes … feeling refreshed and relaxed.

Cloud Metaphor

What would happen if you packed yourself in a cloud? … I would like you to imagine that you have a cloud … packed around your feet and ankles … packing a cloud around your knees … behind your knees … packing a cloud around your thighs … packing a cloud around your hips … giving yourself permission to float backwards and down … into your cloud … listening to my voice and letting go … and dropping down even deeper …

Packing a cloud around your waist and back … under your hips … around your chest and back … feeling the wonderful sensation … of having a cloud … packed under your arms and around your arms … packed around your wrists … hands … fingers … dropping down deeper and deeper into trance … Now I'd like you to have a cloud packed around your neck … the back of your head … around your face … what if you can feel yourself floating … what would it be like, to sink down into your cloud … feeling yourself floating … deeper and deeper … into a profound trance?

We're going to count down … from one to five … each number taking you down deeper and deeper into trance … As we count the numbers … I would like you to imagine … that you can see them in your third eye … just like you were looking at the image of my hand … Let's start with the number one … you can see the number one as a full three-dimensional reality … perhaps you can feel it vibrating … number one … as it vibrates … it takes you down deeper … and deeper … and as the number one slowly sinks below the horizon … you find yourself drifting deeper … and deeper … into trance … letting go … that's right …

And the number two is vibrating in your third eye … it is a different color … I wonder if you can see the color … if you can imagine … that you can see the color … it doesn't matter if you can see it or not … you can imagine you can see it … and you can feel the vibration … the vibration of the number two becomes magnetic … and it attracts all your random thoughts … random voices … random doubts … and worries … all become attracted like a magnet to the number two … and as the number two starts sinking deeper and deeper … below the horizon … you can find yourself drifting down deeper … into trance …

Next … the number three appears floating in front of you … I wonder if you can imagine … that you can see the number three in three dimensions … full color …

and feeling it vibrating … And the number three is sending out gift waves of relaxation … starting from your head … and taking you all the way down to the soles of your feet … number three is soothing you … as you allow your body to relax completely … and as the number three is growing larger … vibrating as it moves along the whole length of your body … and slowly disappearing below the horizon … taking you down deeper … and deeper … into trance …

There are only two numbers left … number two is a polarity … it's vibrating … and it's attracting all the opposite poles … all the dichotomies … bringing them together … the black and white … the masculine and the feminine … allowing them to integrate …it's attracting the guilt and the fear … and the courage and the heroism … it's attracting the pride … feeling of being superior to others … and the worthlessness … the feeling of being inferior to others … All these feelings and any other polarities can become magnetically attracted to the number two … integrating … and dissolving … and as the number two starts floating out into space … further and further away from you … you can let go … and drop down deeper … and deeper … into trance …

The last number could be a five or it could be a one … it doesn't really matter … but that number is growing larger and larger … until it's as large as your whole body … and that number is going to cover you like a blanket … like a soothing … deep … healing blanket … As that number covers you … it starts to feed into your pores, a soothing, golden, balm of energy … a golden nectar … a healing nectar … and you find yourself … drifting deeper … and deeper … and deeper into trance … as you drop down … that golden nectar starts circulating through your whole body … it's a golden, viscous nectar that is slowly healing all the old scars … nourishing … relaxing … it starts circulating and it's going through every single cell … through all your capillaries … through all of your arteries and veins … And the golden nectar is flowing and circulating … healing all the old scars …

And as the golden nectar continues to circulate … you're going to find yourself floating in your cloud backwards and down through time … floating back through the years as if you're floating through a long, dark tunnel … You find yourself flowing back and down … back through the 80s … back through the 70s … soon you will be in your cloud floating over the house that you lived in as a child … and when you are floating over your house, you can let me know by signaling with your left index finger …

177

Good. That's good. It's good to know that your conscious mind is here and your unconscious mind is here as well … it doesn't really matter if your conscious mind does anything at all … it can be here or not … Because your conscious mind needs to recognize that the golden balm is healing the conscious as well as the unconscious levels … That's very good.

ABC Induction:
Effortless learning and ego strengthening

So I would like you to remember what it was like in the first grade. I don't know what the first grade was like where you went to school, but where I went there was a big alphabet up on the board with a capital letter and a small letter, did you all have that? Do you remember the erasers and the smell of the chalk? I don't know about you, but I remember the smell of the perfume my teacher wore, Miss Narber. What about you? I went to a really old school where my desk was the chair for the person in front of me.

I am going to put on a little music, and I would like you to take your pen in your non-dominant hand … using the hand that you wouldn't ordinarily use … what I want you to do … is to begin printing your name really slowly … really carefully … really slowly and carefully printing your name … letter by letter … and as you draw each letter, you may discover that in drawing the straight lines … and circles … you may be curious how you learned that a b was a backwards d … and a d was something like a p … and how did it all work anyway? … there was a time when you didn't know the alphabet … that's right … you didn't know the b was a backwards d or an upside-down p … and all those straight lines and circles didn't mean anything to you at all … You didn't know how to write your name …

And maybe before you learned the alphabet it seemed like such a big job to remember all those letters … all those circles and straight lines … and how they went … and yet now you know it effortlessly … you never even have to think if a b is a backwards d, or an upside down p … right now you can write your name effortlessly … and you can print anything you like … letter by letter … and you might become aware of the sensation … as your pen touches the paper … of a certain sensation deep inside … now I don't know how you know the difference between and "I" or a "U" or a "W" … but is a W an I and a U? Or is it two "U"s? … What is it anyway … to be able to recognize the pattern … and use that to let go … to relax and drop down even deeper …

I don't know if you remember sitting in that chair in the first grade … did your feet touch the ground? … what is it like to sit in a chair where your feet can swing back and forth without touching the ground … what kind of shoes were you wearing? … I don't know if you remember what it would be like to come home from school and to reach up … to the front doorknob … what would that feel like to reach up all the way for the front doorknob … and I don't know if you have ever walked around your block at home … before school or after school … but what it would it be like? … Were there trees, cars? … Was there a side walk? … Was there a certain smell that you remember really well … perhaps a different smell at different times in the year … that's right … and when you were little … maybe five or six years old … it's such a big job … all those letters and what they meant … and how to recognize them … or how to put them in the right order … how would you ever learn to spell all those words? …

And now it's so effortless … you don't have to think about how to spell your name … about which letter comes next … that's right you can deeply, deeply appreciate that there is a part of you that learned the alphabet … effortlessly … and it's there forever … you don't have to worry about it … you don't have to think about how to spell your name the next time you write … you can deeply relax … you can trust that learning is effortless … and is there whenever you need it …

Suddenly you walk by and you see a sign … you don't have to read it … is that an S or a T and then an O and a P and what does that mean? … You just look at a sign and you already know … and you can go so deeply into appreciation … like that little child … and I don't know how you felt on that first day of school … walking in … did your mom bring you? … Were there lots of strange kids you didn't know … or did you know them all already? … did it seem like a strange environment or was it friendly? … and you wanted to do well … you really wanted to do well and do it right … and you wanted to try so hard to do it right … if only you knew what to do … that's right … so what a deep relief to let go … and to relax … and to recognize that you learned it on such a deep level … that you don't have to figure out how to spell your first name … and the sensation of where the pen touches your fingertips … is just a gentle reminder of when you were five years old … six years old.. when you picked up your first pencil … did it have an eraser? … Did the eraser have a certain smell? … Did you have to write between the lines? … that's right …

And what did it feel like to be so little that you could kick your legs in the chair without touching the ground … and you had such a big responsibility … so much to learn … so hard to do it right … so important to do it right … so important to be loved … so important to be loved by your teacher and your parents … important that you did it right … and sometimes it was so important to be bad … to prove that you didn't have to follow the rules … that there was something even more important … and I don't know if you remember a time when it was important to be bad … and you had to show that you could stand up to rules and what that feels like.. and maybe you never had a time like that … it doesn't matter … but you remember … there are memories that you forgot that you remember … certain feelings … and what was it like when you had to get up and go to school on the first day? … Were you eager? Did you jump out of bed? … or were you frightened and not wanting to go? … That's right … that's right …

And what if right now you were able to just magically go back in time … into that first grade class … and see that little person called by your name … sitting in that chair … wanting to do it right … wanting to be smart and be loved … what if you were to go back to that little person now … and let that one know that "you are loved … you are going to make it" … let that little one know that "you are going to make it … and it is going to turn out all right …that you can deeply relax … and can let go of all the worry … and you will learn everything you need" … that's very good, very good … and what if that little boy or little girl from that school were to take you home … back to the old bedroom … however you get there … what if you were to go home with that little one … can you see the wall paper on the walls … or are the walls painted a certain color? … are there curtains on the window? … and what was the bed like? … what if you could feel that bed under you now with the two of you sitting there together … being shown around your old house … and what if you looked into each others eyes … and experienced the recognition of love …

And what if you could feel a golden cord from your heart to that little child's heart … a golden cord filled with golden nectar … pouring in … healing … soothing … golden nectar pouring into every cell … healing the old hurts … releasing and letting go … that's very good … and now what if you change places and you become the little one … and here is this wiser older one from the future sitting on your bed … and you look into these older, wiser eyes … and there is something important to learn … this older one has seen more of life and has a very important message for you … perhaps you can feel that golden cord … so nourishing and filled with nectar … filling every cell of your body … very good … very good … and maybe you have a gift for this older one … something only a fresh young person like you can give … and you can give the older one a gift now … that's very good.. very good … and what if you switched places now … becoming this older one holding this younger child in your arms … loving the child … recognizing the basic goodness and deep purity … and what kind of gift can you give to this child now … that's very good… very good …

Now what if this child could come with you now back into your heart … integrating him now into your heart … letting the memory itself start to dissolve … and the healing goes forwards and backwards through this memory of time … changing everything … that's right … that's very good … very good … and I wonder how you can discover how the heart opens and softens … and when you are ready … slowly … recognize that you haven't gone anywhere at all … and this trance induction and your dream … and the attachment to it … and this sweetness that is there is the sweetness that is HERE … and the sweetness comes from the love that is here right now and has never gone anywhere … that's very good … and whenever you are ready your eyes can open.

ABC Induction:
Effortlessly learning the language
of the spell, so you can break the spell

So you can take this time and make any adjustments … and you can be completely comfortable and relaxed … and it can feel so good to let the body get as comfortable as possible … that's right … and you may find yourself making subtle adjustments so the body can be deeply relaxed … and as everything settles in and drops down … I wonder if you can become aware of a certain sensation in the soles of your feet … and that's a signal that your body and mind are already dropping down … into a deep … alert … comfortable trance …

And I am curious how you will discover … that even as the body drops into deep sleep … and the conscious mind drops into deep silence … that there is an essential awareness that stays very alert … and doesn't go anywhere at all … that's very good … and as that awareness follows these words … I am going to talk to some other part of you … because there are deeper parts of you … something keeps the heart breathing … something keeps the body breathing … what if the conscious mind had to be responsible for every breath … that would be just too much work … you wouldn't have time to do anything else … so there is another part of consciousness … that takes care of the breathing … the heart beating … and the conscious mind can just sink … and let everything drop deeper … that's very good … very good …

And I don't know if you remember what it was like … back when you did not know how to read and write … there was a time when you could pick up a book and just see a lot of straight lines and circles … that didn't have any meaning at all … and at a certain point you started learning … you learned the difference between a "b" and a "d" … and you discovered that a "q" is not a backwards "p" … and a "d" is not a backwards "b" … and somehow, some part of you learned this alphabet … and now perhaps you know … what is a double "u" … is it an I and a you … anyway … even if the conscious mind thinks about double you … where else would <u>you</u> be? … and yet the other part that Knows the alphabet … learned it without the conscious mind … so now if you pick up a newspaper or a book … you no longer have to look at it and go … there is a "b" … and there is a "c" … and is that really a "p" or a backwards "q"? … some part of you can just read it …

So I don't know if you can imagine what it was like the first time you learned to print your name ... you probably had lined paper ... and maybe a pencil ... in which hand did you hold that pencil in? ... and if you could feel that pencil in your hand right now ... as the hand slowly moves ... printing in capital letters ... your name on the page ... letter ... by letter ... that's very good ... you are doing really well ... and I wonder how long it took to learn to do that ... and how did you learn to do that anyway? ... the conscious mind doesn't know ... but some deeper part of you ... which learned the alphabet ...

and knows it now effortlessly ... without thinking at all you can read a page ... and have deep understanding ... and that part of you that has learned so well ... has been learning here as well ... you have been absorbing ... and this absorption happens on a much deeper level than the conscious mind ... and you discover ... just like how you learned to print your name with capital's ... and then you learned how to write with cursive script ... and it seemed at first that you only knew how to write a few words ... three letter words ... dog ... cat ... hat ... and pretty soon ... all those letters ... and at the time when you were real young it seemed ... how could you ever remember all those letters ... but those letters ... how many letters are there in the alphabet? ... and how are you going to remember all of them ... and how are you going to remember how all those words are spelled? ... that's just too big a job for a little boy or girl ... it's too big a job for the conscious mind ...

But somehow it went in ... you may not have had good teachers ... you may not have had a good school ... or you may have had a wonderful teacher ... and a wonderful school ... it doesn't matter ... something inside when you were very little ... so little that you could sit in a chair ... or kick your legs ... I don't remember if you know what that feels like ... to be that little now ... to be able to sit in a chair and kick your legs ... and if you were to look down at your shoes ... I wonder how small they are ... what color are they? ... that's right ... if you were that small ... wearing those little shoes right now ... you have absorbed everything you need ... you can read and write without even thinking ... because this other part of your consciousness is effortlessly absorbing with deep understanding ...

And that little body ... which can kick in a chair ... and hold a pencil ... write big letters between the lines ... that little person that wanted to be good ... wanted to be loved ... wanted to do it right ... that little body started growing ... getting taller ... feet and hands getting bigger ... hair changing ... muscles changing ... but something didn't change … something is exactly the same now as it was back then … you know that … and as this body grows from being a little one not able to reach the floor while sitting in chair … you can notice that the body goes through stages of life … childhood … adolescence … becoming a young adult … and moving into adulthood … and still something not changing … and still the growing … effortlessly … you don't even have to think about the alphabet anymore … now when you read a book or newspaper or magazine … you never have to wonder … how many letters there are in the alphabet … how they all fit together … its effortless … that's right … the body continues maturing … and something doesn't change … something essential …

And you are going to find that everything you have absorbed … you have learned the alphabet … you have discovered in your own experience … how this alphabet called casting a spell creates the trance of "me and my story" … because when you were little … you used to like stories … and I don't know what your favorite story was … or if your mom ever read to you … but sometimes there are favorite stories that you like to hear again and again … and you discover … that you have learned the alphabet for this story … called "me and my life" … and now you are going to find … that the gift … this Silence which has been there all along … is now going to have an alphabet to express itself … that's right …

And when you sit looking at yourself in the form of someone else … and your mind is completely quiet … you are going to find the vocabulary of how to cast a spell … and how to use the vocabulary of casting a spell to break the spell … the vocabulary of the trance … it will show up effortlessly … the Silence will express itself with a brilliance that the conscious mind couldn't possibly figure out … and I don't know if you can imagine what it would be like right now if you were sitting … in anticipation perhaps … as someone you may have never met sits down in front of you … and your mind becomes even more quiet … and you look into each others' eyes … and you see your Self … in the form of someone else … you discover … that here is Consciousness … casting a spell … asking for help to unweave the web of the spell that has been cast … and you find that you know how to spell … you learned it a long time ago … so the conscious mind can relax even more deeply … just like you don't have to get upset when you read a magazine article … you don't have to worry about what the letters are or what they mean … the conscious mind knows … ahh … it can relax down even more deeply.

And so when you are looking into these eyes … that you are calling someone you have never seen … and yet you see something so familiar … you discover … being curious … what is it that you really want … and you find that this open-hearted curiosity … will bring forth from the depths of your own self called another … the spell … and you will know without even thinking … what this spelling really means … and that's very good … and if the conscious mind is trying to follow everything I have said … it may have followed it or not … it doesn't matter … the conscious attention span is so short … it tends to forget what it has followed in the very next moment …

So it doesn't really matter if you have remembered to forget everything you have heard … or if you forget to remember whatever it is that has happened here this evening … that's right … because you already know how to spell … on a level beyond forgetting … and you have already tasted the truth of your Self on a level beyond knowing or not knowing … and you find that you will be true to That ever more deeply … regardless of what appears or disappears … and the deeper you are in love with the truth of your own Self … this will be the gift that will be transmitted … as you look into your own eyes called another …

And so when you leave here this evening … you may find its been such a perfect night … with the moon and the stars … and it can feel so good to sleep so deeply … a sleep that is so deeply restful … and you can sleep that way or not, it doesn't really matter … but if all the stories suddenly dissolve … you may find yourself suddenly sleeping … in a deep restful way … and waking up so refreshed … refreshed and perhaps even forgetting that you had this experience … or remembering it … either way … as your eyes open and your attention comes back to your body and this room … you can find your Self alert, open-hearted … in deep silence … peace … love.

Erickson Group Trance

Once when Milton Erickson was addressing a group of therapists, at the University of Chicago, I believe, these therapists were working very intensely with different emotional and psychological disorders. Milton looked out at the group and said, "You know you are really doing such important work, you are doing so well, and I am going to tell you a story that might help you with your work." And in his own particular way Milton said, "I am curious if, as you listen to my words … if that can be a signal to you … in a way that is very familiar … so that you can recognize that as I tell you this story … that's right … everything … can dissolve. " And when Milton said that to this group of therapists they didn't really know what he was talking about … and some of them thought they understood, and others were confused …

"And you know," he said, "you know what I mean … because you have been listening so carefully … and you know there is a difference between listening and hearing … and I don't know exactly what that difference is … but you know what the difference is … between listening and hearing." And as he said that there were some people in the room carefully taking notes … and others who suddenly started to hear something … that has always been there … but they were hearing it with new ears.

Now … Milton Erickson would never talk about Silence … and what is it like to hear Silence … because that could sound paradoxical for someone like that to say … because no one ever considered *listening to the Silence* … in the depths of your own heart … and so Erickson spoke about something else … "You know … in listening to your clients … and their stories … and their problems and cases … sometimes it can seem like you have heard it all before … and your mind can drift … and sometimes in sessions you may find that you can fall asleep … it doesn't matter … even that can be a signal to your client that maybe the story is boring to both of you …" Now when Milton said this, it surprised a lot of people … and they thought for a moment. "*Fall asleep? … now?* … Well, to fall asleep now …" And some of them felt very nervous about that–" But I have to hear what he is saying … I have to understand"–yet somehow he was talking about listening with the inner ear … to hear something deeper.

Well, there were those who understood … those who thought it amusing … and those who didn't understand at all … and yet what Milton was really saying and telling this group of people … was that it is okay … if your client's story is boring you can go to sleep ... you can rest ... you can listen to the Silence right now ... Well ... some of them got it and some didn't ... "But what I am curious about ..." Milton said, "Is you as a therapist, what is it that you really want? ... Of course, on some level you really want your client to get better ... on some level, you want to make a lot of money ... on some level, you want to be very successful ... on some level, you want to have a happy life ... on some level, you want to be recognized for what a good job you are doing ... you want mommy and daddy to say, 'Yes! You did grow up right, you were right ... Yes, you did a good job ... Yes, you are doing very well in the world ... Yes, you can take care of yourself ...' Yes ... there are all those things ...

"But I am curious ... " he said to these people ..."what if right now you drop into the very depths ... to discover ... what it is you really want ... now as an experiment" he said ... "what if your awareness were just like a little soap bubble ... that is so light it floats down deeper ... and deeper ... inside ... and as your awareness floats down ... deeper and deeper ... what if for a moment your conscious mind stops ... takes a nap ... and a deep part of you ... the part that is listening to the Silence ... that's right ... that part is so nourishing ... it can feel so good ... to let that part ... that's right ... and as you sink in ... for a moment ... what if like a deep-sea diver ...

"I don't know if any of you have ever experienced scuba diving ..." Milton said, "But I once was talking to Lloyd Bridges ... and Lloyd Bridges said, 'When you scuba dive ... you find yourself drifting down ... weightless ... effortless ... deeper ... and deeper into the depths ... and as you find yourself sinking deeper and deeper into the depths ... ' Lloyd Bridges would say, 'You know you can even look up to the surface from the depths ... and I don't know what it would be like for you ... if you were a scuba diver ... diving in ... to the very depths ... what if you could look up ... to the surface ... where consciousness is breaking ... into eddies and waves and ripples ...

"And what if ... as you float in deeper and deeper ... what if you were to ask your conscious mind ... the thinking rational mind ... what do you really want? ... and if you were to do that now ... I wonder what the answer is ... that's right ... that's very good ... and now if you allow yourself to sink down ... much further down from the conscious mind ... and if you were to approach the emotional heart ... and you asked the emotional heart, what do I really want? ... That's right ... that's very good ... and from here ... what if you sink in to the next level of depth ... letting everything go down ... effortlessly ... deep inside ... down where the sunlight doesn't come through the water anymore ... it is so deep and dark ... down into the depths of darkness … all the way into a perhaps unexplored … yet familiar space … and as you allow yourself to melt in there" he said, "You can ask in the very depths of your soul, what do I really want? … and you can ask yourself now … in the depths of your being … what do I really want? … that's right … that's very good."

And what he said to them then was, "You will recognize that your clients will have desires that are in the mental … desires in the emotional … desires in the physical … and all of these desires are ripples and waves from the very depths of what you really want … and you may start in therapy by satisfying a mental desire … or discovering and satisfying an emotional desire … or a physical desire for change … and that might be an appropriate place to play in the shallows but you as a therapist … will always recognize … that as you listen to the Silence … and you recognize … that as you drop into the depths … how the true desire … ripples and waves into the physical, the emotional, and the mental, and you will recognize how each of those waves is a distortion … from the true silent depth of Stillness," and then he said, "You are doing such a good job … and you are going to discover … in working with people here … that the first question is what do you want? … and that you can always find out what is deeper … and what is on the surface … someone may come in and say, "I want freedom," and you may want to go to the surface to find out, what does freedom mean? What does freedom mean really for you? … what does it mean in your relationship? … Is that where you want freedom? … what does it mean in your work? … Is that where you want it? … Or someone may come in and say, "I want freedom," and it resonates all the way down to the silent depths … into the innermost silent recesses … and you will discover effortlessly … how to unravel any trance … and you will discover effortlessly … the direct experience … for yourself … when the trance stops."

Well, when Erickson said that, it was heard with new ears … and somewhere inside … something resonates … beyond the hearing … in the very depths … there is a recognition … that what you really want … is possible right now … is here right now … and the only imaginary obstacle … is your own trance induction …" And when he said this to this group of therapists, they were very surprised and didn't understand what he meant, and so he said, "Create your trance induction right now … give rise to the thought, I am … with your name on it … and notice where this thought … I am Linda … or I am Shakti … whatever the name is … notice where it comes from … notice the results of it … notice how it starts vibrating physically, mentally and emotionally …

Notice the tentacles of identification when 'I am' arises … I am somebody … then notice the identification … what does it mean, mentally, emotionally and physically? … that's right … and then let this trance induction sink back down into the depths of emptiness … where it arose from … and notice the experience … what are you aware of when this trance induction dissolves? … what are you aware of mentally, emotionally, and physically? … and what is even deeper? … that's right …"

And then Erickson looked seriously at all the therapists in the room and said, "You are doing such as good job. You are learning on a very deep level … and your conscious mind can relax and enjoy the process … and you may discover that the conscious mind really wants to serve … and this service will be a dropping … into the depths … and as you work with people … it is going to be effortless … easier and easier … and you will uncover and be curious … how do they create this trance called me and my suffering? … and you will find out what is going on mentally, emotionally and physically … to create the trance of me and my problem … you will also find out, what do they really want? … and when someone says what they want … what if you don't know what that means … and you could discover … what is going on mentally, emotionally, and physically? …

Well, Erickson finished his remarks to this group of therapists … and when he did it was time for the convention to break for lunch … and I don't know … is it possible … that whether your eyes are open or closed … you can still be exploring … to find out how deep are the depths … that's right … so let your eyes open now … as your awareness sinks down to the next level … that's very good.

The Baby Eagle

Stay very awake as you drop deeper. I'll first tell you a story … sometimes stories go in and resonate in places that actually remember it … the beauty of a story is that it works on many levels … so that the conscious mind can hear it … and deeper parts of you hear it simultaneously. Sometimes you know you can be hearing people speak for days on end … but what you really remember is the anecdotes and stories … something that has a deeper flavor. So as you listen to this story, there's nothing to do … you can just relax … and it doesn't matter what goes on … but you may be curious if it's possible for the mind to just relax … it's as if the mind were to melt down to the very soles of your feet … I don't know what that would mean for you … but you might be aware of the sensations in the soles of your feet … the sounds in the room … you might notice that your breathing has already changed … and all that can just settle you into a place … where the commentary slows down and even stops. The discussion you have with yourself can somehow come to a rest … it is kind of like hitting the pause button on the tape recorder.

It's a story about a baby eagle. This baby eagle was in a nest way up on the highest mountain … and this eagle would be very lonely each time that its mother went out to hunt … so every time the mother went out to hunt the baby would say, "Where did she go, I need her … Where has she gone? I'm hungry! What is she doing? … Why isn't she back already? She's been gone so long."

This baby eagle would get so upset … frantic, worried, nervous … angry, hurt. "Where is she? Why isn't she here yet? Why is it taking so long? I'm cold. I need her." And the mother would be soaring down deeply … effortlessly … into the valleys to hunt for food for her baby … and she'd bring the food back and feed the baby. One day she came back and the baby was very irritated and very upset … wondering why she was gone so long? "Where have you been and why did it take so long? I really needed you and I called for you and you didn't answer!" And the mother held the food just out of reach … and the baby eagle reached for the food … and in reaching for the food … fell out of the nest and started to fall … deeper and deeper down toward the valley below.

Well, the baby eagle got very angry … very angry, flapping its wings as hard as it could … it looked up at its mother and started to yell, "How could you do this to me?

191

Look what you've done! Why don't you come and get me? Why don't you help me now? Why don't you help me?" And the baby yelled and screamed at the mother … furiously flapping its wings … looking up at her and falling deeper and deeper into the valley below. When the baby had yelled everything it could yell … cursed her and called her names … feeling this rage completely … suddenly the anger was gone … and an enormous sadness came into this baby eagle … a sadness over the loss … sadness over how the mother could have done this … and the baby started to cry … and as it cried it flapped its wings … and called out for the mother … and sobbing it looked up at its mother … and the mother just circled overhead … and the baby fell further and further … into the valley below …

Well, the baby was just distraught … it cried its heart out … it cried until there were no more tears … and this overwhelming sadness … at having lost the nest … and lost its mother … and "why is she not helping me? … she is just circling up there? … and then … all the tears were gone … and the baby became very afraid … suddenly terror became very real … "My God I am going to die?" And this terror was so deep … it was a bone-chilling terror … so the whole baby's body froze … it couldn't even flap its wings … it just looked at its mother in absolute terror … so terrified it couldn't even scream … just like a silent cry that was too frozen to even get out … and the baby fell deeper.. and deeper … into the valley below.

Well the sense of terror turned into despair … the baby eagle realized that it was hopeless, it is helpless, it is never going to get back to the nest … "I'm not going to make it, I can't fly … its over, there's nothing left." And this despair was like an overwhelming black cloud … which came up on the inside of this baby eagle … and the baby recognized there was nothing left it could do.

It had tried … it had called … it had cried … it had beaten its wings … and there was nothing left to do … and the baby sank even deeper … into this hopeless helplessness … and into a vast emptiness … and as the baby surrendered … and let go … it completely relaxed and gave up the struggle …and the baby eagle's body naturally started pointing with its head down … in the direction it was already falling … and once its head went down in the direction it was already falling … its wings naturally opened up … and without any effort at all … the baby discovered it could soar … soar effortlessly on the gentle currents of air.

Well, the baby soared up in gentle circles … till it was back up to the level of its mother … and now it looked at its mother with a whole different understanding …

everything was melted … overwhelming gratitude started to fill up the baby eagle's heart … and as the baby looked at its mother with this overwhelming gratitude … there was a recognition and a trust … that somehow deepened in an unknowable way … then they looked at the nest and realized it was quite small … and not quite as comfortable as they had remembered … and that in fact another impulse came … that it was time to build its own nest … to discover its own flight.

Now I don't know what relationship you feel with this story … but I will be curious if you will discover … how effortlessly you can turn your head in the direction you are already falling … how quickly and how gently … you begin to discover what has always already been there … there is nothing to add … there is nothing to make … there is nothing to transform … there is nothing to change …there is nothing you have to do anything with … it is discovering what is already there resting deeper and more deeply still …

Vishnu and the Tea Cup

What I say may or may not make sense. And it doesn't really matter. But if right now, you just become aware of the body for a moment … we will become aware of the body and then go inward. So just noticing how the body is touching the ground. And you might be aware of how your feet are touching the ground … and there might be a certain sensation in the soles of your feet … and that's a signal that something is already changing … you are already dropping into a different state … you may be very aware of the sounds in this room … the sound of my voice …and a very subtle sensation deep inside … and that subtle sensation deep inside may attract you … it might become more interesting than the sounds … and it might take you to a very different place … and you might notice that your breathing has changed … that's right … and that is a signal … that you are dropping even deeper inside … and you may discover that you can let go of the sensation … and find what's even deeper underneath it … very good … it can be such a relief for the mind to finally rest … relax … and drop down … as your awareness is sinking deeper … and deeper … very safe … sweet … space … that's very good … very good.

I'm going to ask you now … to try this little experiment … you are going to ask different parts … your mind … your emotions … what is it that you really want in order to be happy? … so let's start in your mental body … asking your thoughts … what is it that you really want to be happy? … and notice what the thoughts say you need for you to be happy … that's very good … and now let your awareness drop out of the thoughts and into the emotions … a place where you feel sadness or anger … or fear or hurt … ask the place of emotions … what is it that you really want? … what will make you happy? … very good, that's very good … and now you may find that as you sink deeper … beyond the emotions … sinking all the way in to the very core … allowing yourself to float down into a vast depth … into a place of deep wisdom … deep wisdom that's always there … and now asking the very core of your being … what is it that you want? … what is it that will make you happy? … that's very good, very good … you may discover that as you rest even deeper … that you can float down into a depth of peace … that's right …

I'm going to tell you a little story … and as I tell you a story you can listen or not … it doesn't really matter … but whether you hear the words or you don't hear the words … something in the very depths is teaching you … is leading you … is taking you down … even deeper.

One day … once upon a time … a long time ago … and as you hear these words they may be familiar or not … you may use the words as a signal to drop down to an even deeper peace … there was once a young man who was willing to die for the truth … and in this courage and willingness … Vishnu appeared … and the God Vishnu said to the man, "I'm very happy with you. I grant you a wish. Any wish that you want will be fulfilled. And this young man said to Vishnu, "What I really want is … I want to learn the secret of Maya." And Vishnu said, "Oh, no, not that … ask for something else … ask for a long life … ask for wealth … ask for horses or elephants … don't ask me about that." And the young man said, "No, that's really what I want, I must learn the secret of Maya … Please tell me." And Vishnu said "Okay, if that's really what you want I will tell you … but before I do … if you just walk over to that well there … and get me a cup of water before we begin …

And the young man went over to the well … and as he was getting the water for Vishnu … a young girl had come from the village to also draw water from the well … and when he looked in her eyes … and she looked into his … he couldn't believe it … instant recognition … deepest love … he just couldn't believe it … his soul mate … the perfect one … the one he had been waiting for his whole life … his heart just exploded … he didn't know what to do … the way she looked … the way she smiled at him … her eyes … just perfect … and she looked back at him and saw the same thing … her soul mate … the one that she had been waiting for … he looked right … he smiled right … his heart was open … and they just deeply … deeply … fell in love …

And she said listen … I don't know what's happened here … what should we do? And he said, "I want to marry you … I love you … I've been searching for you my whole life. You are what I have been waiting for … Please let me come and meet your father and ask his permission to marry you!"

And so this young girl … took this man back to her house … and it turned out that her father was the head man of the village … and when they knocked on the door … and the family opened the door … they took him in like the long lost son … they also recognized him … as though he had always belonged there … and they said, "Come in! Come in! Where have you been?" … And he said, "I have fallen in love with your daughter and I want to marry her" … and they were very, very happy

... and the father said, "Well, you can marry her ... but on one condition ... since I am the head man in this village ... I don't want her to leave ... so if you are willing to stay here in this village ... I will provide you both with a farm and a house ... if you can agree to that ... then you can certainly marry my daughter" ... and the young man readily agreed ... and so they planned the wedding ... the whole town came ... people saw them and said, "Look at this perfect couple ... they look like they were meant for each other ... they fit so harmoniously!"

And after they were married they moved onto their farm ... and they started to have babies ... they had a little daughter ... then they had a son ... and then another daughter ... and their life seemed so full and productive ... the fields were growing ... the children were growing ... the animals were growing ... their life together was blissful ...

And then one day ... there was an enormous thundering in the mountains ... it was so strong and deep that everyone knew ... a flash flood was coming ... Quick, grab the children! We have to get out of here! And the man grabbed the youngest girl and put her on his shoulders ... he held onto the boy's hand ... his wife had the other daughter ... and he held onto her hand and they started running ... and an enormous wall of muddy water came rushing down from the mountains ... it destroyed the fields ... drowned the animals ... washed away their house ... and they were running ... and the water was up to their knees ... and then it was up to their hips ... still running ... then the little girl fell off of his shoulders ... and he reached for her ... and in reaching for her, he dropped the other one and let go of his wife's hand ... and they all got washed away ... washed into the flood ... washed into the waters ... and this man just didn't know what to do ... his heart was broken ... he had suddenly in an instant lost everything ... the farm was gone ... the children were gone ... his beautiful wife was gone ... everything was gone ... his heart was torn open ... and he started crying ... inconsolably crying over his loss ...

And then an amazing thing happened ... as his tears dropped into the muddy water ... the water started to clarify ... it became very still and clear ... and then the young man noticed ... his tears were actually dropping into a cup of water ... and at that moment ... he looked up ... and Vishnu said, "What took you so long ... where is my cup of water?" and in that way, Vishnu taught the young man the secret of Maya.

And when he had understood this ... the heart that had been split open created a gateway ... and the man resolved to turn his back on suffering ... to discover what doesn't come and go ... to discover the absolute truth.

So I don't know what this story might mean to you … or how you will take it? But be curious about how you will discover the depths … in more and more subtle ways … and to just tell the truth about which direction you are pointed in … Are you going outward? … Or inward? … Into the mind? … Or down towards the source? … It is really very simple … and you will discover it effortlessly … that's very good.

So whenever you are ready your eyes can open … and you can find yourself not moving at all … and yet appearing to be present here.

PART FIVE

Ego Transcendence and
the Enneagram

Egoic Identification *vs* Self Realization

Ego State	Self
• Suffering	• Bliss
• Duality: subject and objects	• Non dualistic, Oneness
• Alway doing and a doer	• No doer
• Choices	• Choicelessness
• Effort	• No effort
• Afraid of being alone, alone = separate	• No other, alone = All One
• Feeling of Helplessness	• Sense of help everywhere
• Control issue: *"who is in control?"*	• Surrender

In the egoic state we presuppose that "I" refers to a separate entity called by our name, and that this is the "doer." Arrogance arises in believing that "I can do" and "you should do", and this leads to a search for knowing the right thing to do, and the creation of a belief in a superego which judges what is done as good or bad. In this state we are continually confronted with making choices, deciding what is the right thing to do. We call this our "freedom of choice."

True Freedom is discovered in giving up all choices, in total surrender. This is exactly the opposite of what we are conditioned to believe. We have always felt freedom was having a choice. Yet in surrender, something else takes charge; an awareness, intelligence, and love, deeper than the conscious mind, functions through the body spontaneously. The deeper the surrender to this Unknown Source, the deeper the Bliss.

The Enneagram uncovers the subconscious identification with name and form. It reveals where consciousness has identified itself as "me." The tendency of the mind is to land in the belief that this is "me", as subconscious patterns are uncovered. The possibility is to realize the Truth and remain identified as That. In the firm commitment to be true to the Truth of Self, there is a burning of the fixation as subconscious tendencies arise in this exposure

Enneagram of Character Fixation

If you fully integrate what you have read so far, you will have the tools and insights to be a very powerful agent of change. After years as a successful therapist using the tools of NLP and Hypnosis, I felt that there was still something missing in my practice. Learning the enneagram in the early 1980's changed everything. It added a depth of precision in diagnosing the clients in front of me.

Besides aiding my clinical work it was essential in my relationship with my partner. Without my partner and I knowing our fixations our relationship would never have lasted.

While it is not scope of this book to present the enneagram in full, this brief explanation will hopefully wet your appetite for more. My book, *Fixation to Freedom:*

The Enneagram of Liberation, gives a full map of the system with close detail to each fixation. My approach is very different from the Enneagram of Personality and takes you into the essence of true character and the mask of character fixation that underlies all personality. Please do not assume that the Enneagram of Character Fixation is the same system leading to the same outcomes as the Enneagram of Personality.

Here we will skim the surface to show the power of this language of self-examination. For the enneagram is a language to describe the deep structures of the egoic mind. If your interest includes self-inquiry, self-realization and the liberation potential inherent in a human life then the enneagram of character fixation can be an essential key.

"The personal entity which identifies its existence with
life in the physical body and calls itself "I" is the ego. The physical
body, which is inherently inert, has no ego sense. The Self, which is
pure consciousness, has no ego sense. Between these two there
mysteriously arises the ego sense, which is the "I" thought.

This ego, or personal identity is at the root of all suffering in life.
Therefore, it is to be destroyed by any means possible … this is
Liberation or Enlightenment, or Self-realization."

Ramana Maharshi

Ramana Maharshi's suggested method of cutting the egoic knot is called Self-Inquiry. This is the essence of the innermost teachings that originate in the Indian stream and later give rise to the Buddha's same realization and suggested method. This method can be best characterized as a silent mind discovering its source.

A silent mind is a mind free of entanglements. A silent mind has given up the struggle to be right, to know, to do and to have. In the depth of realization all entanglements and struggles are burned in the recognition of their non-reality.

Traditionally, self-inquiry is described as a process of the mind turning within to discover, "Who am I?" "Am I this body? Am I these thoughts? Am I these feelings?" As this silent mind notices the arising of the thought "I" it follows this thought of "I" to its source where it dissolves and the true "I" shines forth.

Both the Hindu and Buddhist method end with sudden awakening. The path to this end varies as fits the circumstances of the times and the ripeness of the soul. At the end of the path, the same Teacher is always waiting.

The Enneagram of Character Fixation as we now know it is the most precise description that we have of the knot of ego that must be cut. It shows us that consciousness has crystallized itself in the physical, mental or emotional body. It shows us the tests that must be passed, the qualifications that must be there, to end the searching and begin the finding.

These tests show up mentally, emotionally, physically and in the situational body. The situational body is a bubble of perception. It reflects the fluctuations of mind projected in the form of your specific life circumstance. What appears as one's family, friends, relationships, work, survival, sex, all appear in the situational body. This is the magic theater where we are tested and initiated.

The tests are the tests of character as opposed to character fixation. In a metaphorical sense, the holy ideas of the fixation are in combat with the passions of the fixation for the ownership of your soul. Only you can choose. Your choices have enormous repercussions. If you choose selfishly you are thrown into circumstantial hell. If you choose Truth, Freedom, Love over your personal comfort, over your fixated identity, you have chosen character that destroys character fixation and leads to a deep essential Peace that is transcendent of circumstance. Love is seen everywhere. You are led to the truth of your nature that is beyond essence.

Character Fixation is hiding the absence of character. By true character I mean the soul's own integrity and essence. Choosing essential kindness over the fixated imitation of kindness, may not appear to be kind at all. It does not care about appearance. It expects nothing in return. Fixated kindness cares very much about how it looks and what's in it for me.

The tests will appear at every fixation. However, the place where you are fixated is the place where you are most asleep and most unwilling to give up your crutches and excuses. This is the great gift of the Enneagram. It points you in the direction of its own destruction.

The Enneagram is a precise description of the knot of ego. The Enneagram perfectly describes the false "I" of the "doer" the "knower" and the "enjoyer of pleasures." The Enneagram is a mirror in which you can see who you are not. The story of the fixation is the fixation's interpretations of its mind-flux in relationship with the appearance of "other."

Every fixation is busy either doing something, or worrying about what to do or judging something that has been done. The precise descriptions of the doer are the keys to recognize both the futility of "doing" and the possibility of the dawning of the "end of doing."

From direct experience with the Enneagram as a frame, we discover that all egoic "doing" is covering the avoidance of the experience of terror. The doubt of the six fixation can be a Dharma bell ringing to say, "You are avoiding the experience of terror in this moment." In this understanding doubt itself becomes an aid to facing what the fixation is avoiding, and in this way uncover latent subconscious identification with form. By form I mean either physical, mental or emotional bodies and conditions.

Once there is a willingness to drop into the terror and despair that is at the heart of all fixation, you will discover the black hole. Surrendering here, to the certainty of death, is the gateway to freedom.

All ego, every fixation, is an attempt to buffer against the possibility of falling into this black hole. Every fixation desires pleasure and avoids pain. Once these patterns are seen as mechanical and habitual, they can be discarded in the search for who you really are. You realize that what you are hungry for is essence and what you are settling for is either an idea of security, or comfort, or intense physical stimulation. In this recognition there arises a willingness to surrender everything to essence.

Every fixation describes patterns of knowing and ignorance. In the rejection of both knowing and ignorance alert not-knowing appears as the mind without fluctuation.

Every soul is longing for home. Recognizing this longing is spiritual maturity. This longing for home, Peace, Freedom, Love is the only true desire. Until this desire is realized, it is siphoned off into the desires of the fixation. The desires of the fixation, the passions that run the fixation, are the mind fluctuations that create the veiling of home.

Once you are willing to no longer play out the habitual suffering of identifying yourself as a fixation, you are ready to cut the knot and discover the truth. This involves an uncovering of the deeper subconscious motivations that have been running the fixated behaviors, thoughts and feelings.

Eventually, there is the realization that all the strategies of fixation are attempts to avoid the certainty of death. When you are ready to dive into the black hole, to face your worst nightmares, to give up all idea of yourself as a personal entity, then you are ready to face death and discover what dies. In this willingness to face death totally, the mind naturally drops into silence. Through the portals of death, realization is waiting.

Once the realization has dawned, there is not necessarily a burning of all latent subconscious identification with form. The Enneagram will be there as a guide so that if latent identifications arise, you won't be fooled by them. For example, when doubt arises, you know that this is not fresh insight. When lust arises, you know that this is not just "being in the moment." In this way, as long as the body breathes, the Enneagram is there as a mirror for the breath to see itself. A silent mind and self-inquiry, wedded with the Enneagram, make the rarest gift of all available to everyone.

The Obsessive/Compulsives

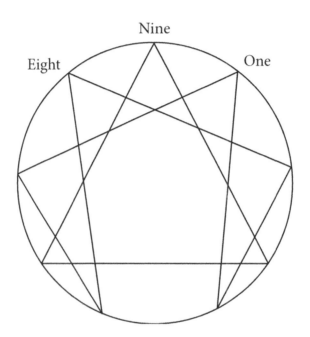

Nine: The core anger point

- The avoidance of anger as the ideal.
- Passive-aggressive as a strategy to avoid and express anger.
- Childhood environment: being a "back grounded" good child.
- The path of love and waking up.

Eight: The externalized anger point

- Acting out and "lust for life" as a strategy to fend off self-deadening.
- Vengeance and "laying trips" as the defense of a wounded child.
- The path of innocence and truth.

One: The internalized anger point

- The perfectionist personality and the expression of resentment.
- Role of the super-ego in defending against "bad."
- Toilet training, anal contraction and anal-genital neuroses.
- Path of forgiveness, serenity and perfection

POINT 9: THE CORE ANGER POINT

Chief Feature:	Indolence
Passion:	Laziness
Idealization:	I am Comfortable
Talking style:	Saga
Trap:	Seeker
Defense Mechanism:	Self-Narcotization
Avoidance:	Conflict
Dichotomy:	Believer/Doubter

Sub-Types:	
Self-Preservation:	Appetite
Social:	Participation
Sexual:	Union

What is immediately noticeable is the absence of anger. Often appearing sweet, and slow and syrupy, the Indolent point is almost always feeling some anger that gets expressed in a passive/aggressive way. These are the people who have a hard time saying "no," but if feeling coerced will be late and stubborn in following through. Pressure, particularly around either time, or money or cleanliness, is perceived as aggression. Nines will often " space-out," which can be perceived as a blank look or clouding of the eyes.

As little children, these people were caught between compliance and rage. With one leg in the conformist side of the Enneagram, and one in the non-conformist, the nine responds by non-action and mechanization of life. This is the place of self-deadening through routine. This is the place of habit and habitual routines that run the life. Everything, from which restaurant to go to and what to order, to toilet and sex habits can become routinized and mechanical. The talking style tends towards end-less tangents and sagas. Being listened to becomes an important unconscious issue.

When feeling strong anger, the Indolent character tends to store it in the neck and back, and to self-inflict injuries. This is the home of orthopedic problems and "accidents." As conflict is strongly avoided it is extremely hard for the indolent char-acter to actually become angry or assertive or confrontive in the moment. At best it becomes relived at a later, safer time. The feeling here is that if truly unleashed, the anger would be so devastating as to be potentially deadly. The build-up of unexpressed rage is felt like a pressure cooker. The self-compromise of the indolent character is the decision that it is best to avoid the anger and ignore the pressure.

These people can truly reflect all points of view and often feel themselves getting lost in, or merging into, the lives of others. There is often a sense of loss of boundaries between self and other.

POINT 8: THE EXTERNALIZED ANGER POINT

Chief Feature:	Vengeance
Passion:	Lust
Idealization:	I am Competent
Talking Style:	Laying Trips
Trap:	Justice
Defense Mechanism:	Denial
Avoidance:	Weakness
Dichotomy:	Puritan/Hedonist
Sub-types:	
Self-Preservation:	Satisfactory Survival
Social:	Friendship
Sexual:	Possession/Surrender

If the nine is noticeable by the absence of anger, the eight is the home of the abusive character. This is the place of expressed rage and blame; the home of the bully, the bigot and the outlaw. Eights are often loud and demanding and short-tempered. They can be, and often enjoy being verbally abusive. This is the place of defiance of authority and living by a personal code without regard to societal rules or regulations.

As children eights were the "bad" boys and girls. Eights were often punished for things they didn't do and got away with things they should have been punished for. This creates a penchant for blaming the world in order to justify the eight's "innocence." The world is often perceived as a jungle with the threat of random violence either on the street or at home. These were kids who lost their innocence at a very early age. They had to appear mature and tough in order to survive and therefore developed a pushy, abrasive exterior to protect a damaged, frightened child. Showing weakness is avoided at all costs and the appearance of competence becomes the shield to ward off attacks. Although, since denial is the defense, the eight would love to fight with you about the truth of that last sentence, since they believe they "truly are" competent. Often, the eight would also love to fight with you about justice for the under-dog. The issue of justice, and "being right" often justifies the eight's violent behavior.

POINT 1: THE INTERIORIZED ANGER POINT

Chief Feature:	Resentment
Passion:	Anger
Idealization:	I am Righteous
Talking Style:	Preaching
Trap:	Perfection
Defense Mechanism:	Reaction Formation
Avoidance:	Anger
Dichotomy:	Rigid/Sensitive
Sub-types:	
Self-Preservation:	Worry
Social:	Inadaptability
Sexual:	Jealousy

If "Eights" were the bad boys and girls expressing rage, "Ones" were the good boys and girls. They were punished properly for the things they did wrong and were rewarded for being good. These people have been described as having lost the battle of potty training. The anger is stored in the tightly wrapped musculature and is often a reflection of tightness in the anal area. Anal-genital eroticism is often bound up in the dichotomy that the "Ones" experience as the constant condition of life.

This is the place of the most developed super-ego. Where the "Nine" feels anger and goes to sleep, and the "Eight" experiences anger and acts out, the "One" experiences anger and processes it. The anger is judged and shunted through the system. Expressing anger is not considered proper behavior, and therefore the "One" suppresses it. Unfortunately, this unexpressed charge later leaks out as resentment and judgment. The "One" can be cutting in humor and a perfectionist in judging his own and others' performance. Since the passion is anger and the avoidance is anger, this is the place of conflicted polarization. It is often the case that the superego "dissolves" in alcohol" allowing the "One" to shed the puritan pole and express sexuality.

The "One" is the natural home of the "Plains Preacher" and the small businessman. There is a belief in hard work and possibility of making it in life through earnest sustained effort. The worry of the "One" is anger projected into the future.

The Hysterics/Image Points

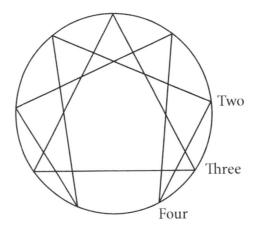

Three: The core hysteric point
- Competence as a mask for unlovability.
- Deceit and the loss of self in production.
- Libidinizing product.
- Path of unmasking and dharma.

Two: The externalized hysteric
- Giving to get: issues of extracting self-worth.
- Pride and the perfect woman syndrome
- The problems with being "daddy's little girl."
- The path of humility and freedom.

Four: The interiorized hysteric
- Melancholy and melodrama as life signals.
- The self-created personality. The artist/dancer.
- Loss of essential love acted out through loss of the father.
- The path of origin and equanimity.

POINT 3: THE CORE IMAGE POINT

Passion:	Deceit
Idealization:	I am Successful
Talking Style:	Propaganda
Trap:	Efficiency
Defense Mechanism:	Identification
Avoidance:	Failure
Dichotomy:	Overactive/Fantasy
Sub-types:	
Self-Preservation:	Security
Social:	Prestige
Sexual:	Male/Female

This is the place of gaining self-worth through production. Just as in the core anger point what is noticed is an absence of anger, here in the core hysteric what is noticed is an absence of hysteria. This is the place of cool competence and maximum efficiency in getting the job done. These were the children who very early in life realized that they could not be loved for themselves but rather for the product they produced. This often created child prodigies, class leaders, over-achievers and head cheerleaders.

In the fear points we notice a leakage of energy into the mental body, in the anger points the leakage is in the physical body, and here in the hysterics the leakage is in the emotional body. This is the natural home of the libidinization of product. This is the core of the seduction by images of the world.

While the three can achieve the appearance of the perfect home or family, there is often difficulty in sustained deep vulnerable tenderness. Since the defense is identification, the three acts as if he or she is "the doctor" or the "football star." There is often a loss of quotes as the three propagandizes about what they do, and how well they are doing, as if what they do is who they are. The trap of efficiency will create poly-phasic type A behavior as well as the possibility of the "ruthless climb to the top."

POINT 2: THE EXTERIORIZED IMAGE POINT

Passion:	Pride
Idealization:	I am Helpful
Talking Style:	Giving Advice
Trap:	Will
Defense Mechanism:	Repression
Avoidance:	Needs
Dichotomy:	Militant/Libertine
Sub-types:	
Self-Preservation:	Me-First
Social:	Ambition
Sexual:	Seduction/Surrender

This is the natural home of daddy's little girl. The idealized myth of the American and particularly the Southern woman is the graceful, charming, hostess who is also the behind-the-scenes helper and the perfect mother while running the household as an efficient ship.

As little girls there is often a sense of winning the competition with mommy for daddy's love. There is often the sense of having had an idyllic childhood as "the two" basked in her cuteness and her tricks for winning affection.

While the engine that runs the machine is pride, the two is almost never consciously aware of this as an issue. Since the defense is repression of one's own needs in favor of another, the two is often ignorant of her true needs. Where the eight will revel in his lust, the two will often be truly unaware that pride has anything to do with her behavior.

While there is often the sense of giving oneself away for the benefit of others, the giving of the two as been described as an extracting process. Extracting self-worth from another by giving yourself away, almost always results in bitterness, resentment and blame. You can never really make up to a two for all that she has done for you.

The holy idea of freedom is often present as a fantasy of being alone on a tropical island with no one to take care of except oneself.

POINT 4: THE INTERIORIZED IMAGE POINT

Passion:	Envy
Idealization:	I am Elite
Talking Style:	Lamentation
Trap:	Authenticity
Defense Mechanism:	Introjection
Avoidance:	Feeling Lost
Dichotomy:	Analytic/Disoriented
Sub-types:	
Self-Preservation:	Dauntless
Social:	Shame
Sexual:	Competition

The natural home of dancers, artists and workshop junkies, often these are people who are continually working on themselves. The home of cosmetic surgery and the "perm," the four loves to dress with unique style. Hours can be spent on make-up that looks "natural" and compliments an expensive, natural fiber, layered look.

Where the two won daddy's love, the four feels the loss of the father. Both male and female fours experience daddy's loss and internalize the experience to mean that "there is something wrong with me." The four then creates herself or himself to be the person that daddy would love. The feeling of the loss and the defense of introjection create the natural "drama queens" of the world. Feeling themselves to be "marked" by the loss, and therefore unique, the four can develop a sense of elitism and that "normal rules don't apply to me." And yet driven by the passion of envy, the four feels a deep lack of self-worth, and a need for constant comparison with others. An exquisite cut flower in a fine crystal vase, beautiful but already dying and cut off at the root, the four revels in her melancholy.

The talking style of lamentation is often heard as the four reminisces about the past or longs for the impossible future. The loss of the father gets recreated over and over again in an unending emotional drama.

The Paranoid/Schizophrenics

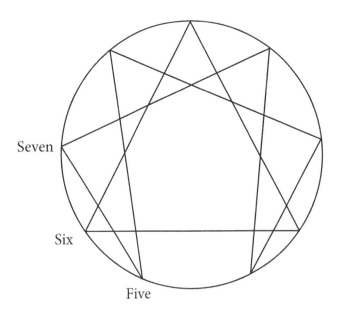

Six: The core fear point

- Mental activity as an avoidance of fear.
- Hierarchy and structure to keep the world safe.
- Having to replace the father at an early age and the neuroses of seeing through things.
- The path of courage and faith.

Seven: The exteriorized fear point

- Planning the future as an avoidance of the present.
- The con man and gluttony for experience.
- The pampered peter pan.
- The path of sobriety and holy work.

Five: The interiorized fear point

- Wizard mind and flat affect.
- Building walls when there are no defenses.
- Withholding and the overly-intrusive parent.
- The path of non-attachment and omniscience.

POINT 6: THE CORE FEAR POINT

Passion:	Doubt
Idealization:	I am Loyal
Talking Style:	Setting Limits
Trap:	Security
Defense Mechanism:	Projection
Avoidance:	Deviance
Dichotomy:	Pushy/Surrender
Sub-types:	
Self-Preservation:	Warmth
Social:	Duty
Sexual:	Strength and Beauty

In the Fear Points we find the crystallization in the Mental Body. These people have a habit of staying in the mental body to avoid the feelings of fear. The passion is doubt, and there is a level of doubt in everything. This is the home of "internal dialogue," generating self-doubt and then projecting it out onto the world. As deep emotions may come out as deviant, they are avoided by creating structures in the mental body. This again is projected onto the world as the perceived need for structure, as bad as it may be, to keep the chaos in bounds. Duty is then an important issue for all Sixes, as they see themselves as loyal and they perceive the need for everyone to do his job to keep the world in order.

As children there may have been a family secret and often a weak, incompetent or absent father. The family secret created a war-zone mentality with constant scanning to be sure no one found out. The child felt the need to substitute for the father at some point and knew s/he was incompetent for the job. These two factors combine to create a sense of unreality, as the six can see behind the scenes, as well as felt incompetence.

Sometimes there is a sense of being an impersonator at the job. This also can create behavioral stuttering, with many false starts and few completions. The body is seen as an instrument of the mind, with the ego disassociating from the emotions and body. The home of black-belt karate champions, chess masters, Hitler, Freud and Woody Allen, the sub-types include a wide variety of apparent manifestation.

POINT 7: THE EXTERNALIZED FEAR POINT

Passion:	Gluttony
Idealization:	I am OK
Talking Style:	Stories
Trap:	Idealism
Defense Mechanism:	Rationalization
Avoidance:	Pain
Dichotomy:	Superior/Inferior
Sub-types:	
Self-Preservation:	Extended Family
Social:	Martyr
Sexual:	Suggestibility

The natural home of the extended families and "flower power," the seven, avoids the fear of six by "magical thinking." Just as Peter Pan teaches the Darling children that "thinking good thoughts can make you fly," the seven dwells on good thoughts and cheering up those around to avoid fear and pain. Thinking can be laterally tangential, making often brilliant connections and insights, but quickly bored with retracing steps and going deeper.

These are the charmers and con-men of the Enneagram, often with a charming witty style that speaks of class and ease of life. Cary Grant, a poor cockney, desperate to make it out of the slums, is a classic example of the seven putting on a style to slide by in the world.

The fascination for new ideas and gluttony for experience makes it difficult for a seven to stay focused in one place for very long. There is a continual desire to change jobs and locations to discover new insights and highs. This also makes the act of choosing very difficult. To choose one is to die to the many.

Pain is avoided by moving away and rationalized by making every move a part of a larger, divine plan. These people can be cosmic travelers, sampling psychedelics, living frugally as health food devotees, and cheering up those they come in contact with.

POINT 5: THE INTERIORIZED FEAR POINT

Passion:	Avarice
Idealization:	I Know
Talking Style:	Treatise
Trap:	Observer
Defense Mechanism:	Isolation
Avoidance:	Emptiness
Dichotomy:	Social/Anti-Social
Sub-types:	
Self-Preservation:	Home
Social:	Totem
Sexual:	Confidence

The five avoids the core fear by going inside and withdrawing from contact with the world. These are people who can appear to have a very flat affect, often with the ability to disappear into the background. The five often loves to be the fly on the wall at social engagements. With not much outward defense, the Five feels raw from contact with the outside world. This is the place of beards and tender, sensitive skin. Rashes and allergies and phobias of germs can be found here. These were usually children with an over-intrusive parent. The only retreat from the parent's prying eyes and demands for compliance and love was to retreat inward. Some of the deepest, most tender feelings can be found in fives, if the five trusts you enough to let you in, and if you don't intrude.

This is the natural home of investigative reporters and eccentric inventors. This is the place of phantasmagoric thinking a la Tolkien. This is also the place of fly-paper minds and collectors who love to categorize their collections. In the sexual sub-type you can find great actors and actresses like Meryl Streep and William Hurt. The social/anti-social dichotomy will determine the degree and kind of contact in the world, as the five can be a hermit or a sports newscaster.

Enneagram Movement of Energy

The Anger Points are crystalized in the physical body. They typically move against the following:

8	9	1
being controlled	discomfort	personal desires
authority	anger	chaos
injustice	trusting the self	spontaneity
rules	being told what to do	relaxation
confinement	own opinions	fun/ play
opposition	own needs	bodily impulses
boredom	focus	flexibility
environment		anger
tenderness		
weakness		

The Image Points are crystalized in the emotional body. They typically move toward the following:

2	3	4
people	tasks	specialness
positive strokes	doing	drama
service	success	deep feelings
other's needs	competition	suffering
approval	efficiency	the unique

important people	prestige	refinement
limelight	workaholic	relationships
relationships	successful others	exclusiveness
		the arts

The Fear Points are crystalized in the mental body.
They typically move away from the following:

7	6	5
pain	fear	people
negativity	danger	feelings
seriousness	authority	contact
boredom	uncertainty	conformity
commitment	trust	emptiness
hierarchy	deviance	overstimulation
single interest		not knowing
		conflict

Exercises *for* Ego Transcendence *and* Uncovering Character Fixation

Repeating Questions

- The following questions can be used in dyads, or as individual inquiry.
- They are best used as repeating questions: where one person asks the question, while remaining in Awareness, Emptiness and Love.
- The other person responds without editing, just allowing whatever response wants to come up. After a while the conscious mind will fall away and allow the unconscious to answer spontaneously and unedited.
- The first person repeats the same question, allowing the inquiry to uncover subtler and subtler layers of hidden subconscious identification with fixation.
- You may find that particular questions are stronger for you. Use the one that you feel a reaction to.
- There is no right or wrong answer. This intent of this inquiry is to expose the subconscious thoughts and motivations of the character fixation. You are simply awake, discovering how you have created the trance of suffering. Once you know how you put yourself to sleep, you can choose to be awake.

Fear Point: All fears of safety and survival are because you think you are a body. Bliss is on the other side of what you are afraid of.

Part I

- *What are you avoiding? What do you avoid?*
- *What do you avoid doing? What do you avoid feeling?*
- *What do you do to be safe?*
- *What does fear and doubt stop you from?*
- *How do you know when you are avoiding the direct experience of fear?*

Part II

- *Close your eyes. Sink into Awareness, Emptiness and Love.*
- *What if it is all a trance, and drops away, and you are fresh in the moment?*
- *What if you decided to never hide or run from fear again?*
- *What have you realized?*

Repeating Questions

Anger Point: Here one believes that willful control and anger are necessary for good orderly direction. Giving up control is believed to be a sign of weakness, laziness, or an invitation to be controlled by someone else. True surrender happens in the realization that there is a deeper Beingness which lives this life. In giving up control to That, there is Bliss. The deeper the surrender, the deeper the Bliss.

Part I
- *Why is it important to be in control?*
- *How do you stay in control?*
- *How do you stay in control in the areas of survival? sexual? relationships?*
- *What is the cost of being in control?*

Part II
- *Close your eyes. Drop into Awareness, Emptiness and Love.*
- *What if it is all a trance, and drops away?*
- *What if you decided to never play this game of control again?*
- *What have you realized?*

Repeating Questions

Image Point: Here there is an attempt to create oneself in an image that will be lovable. So rather than being Love, it is a search for Love. In the search for Love there is the sellout to the idea of Love, to the idea of what one should look like, act like, think like in order to get Love.

Part I
- *How do you sell out for love?*
- *How do you create an image of what you think is required to be loved?*
- *What do you think you need to be successful?*
- *What do you expect to get in return for all that you have given to others?*

Part II
- *Close your eyes. Sink into Awareness, Emptiness and Love.*
- *What if it is all a trance, and drops away?*
- *What if you decided to never sell out for love again?*
- *What have you realized?*

Exercise: Nesting Pattern

Dyad:

- One person finds any negative emotion. If you can not find a negative emotion remember a time when you felt one, and allow yourself to have the experience of it.
- Find out what is underneath it. Diving into it, experiencing it fully, and finding what is deeper.
- You want to stay with the emotion until you can let it deepen, and sink all the way through the different layers of the emotional body, through the black hole, and beyond.
- The tendency will be to come out into the physical body, or to loop up into the mental body. It is important to make distinctions between the mental and emotional body, between the physical and the emotional body.
- When attention goes out to the physical or up into the mental, pace and lead back to the emotional body:

It is as if there is an imaginary core at the center that the whole thing is wrapped around, and that is where the emotional body is resonating. You may ask, 'What is under the fear?', and they may suddenly be are aware of their breathing or tightness, and say, 'My neck is tight.' This is coming out into the physical body, going lateral instead of down.

If you say, 'What is underneath the fear?' and they say, "I have this sense that I can't do anything anymore." That is a thought. They have looped back up into the thinking. So you just acknowledge it, "Yes very good, you can think that. Then drop back into the feeling."

This is an experiment, let's see what happens. It may work, it may not, it does not matter, you will learn something either way.

But what happens at the end after you have gone through?

Find out. What happens? Is there an end? Stay there. Open your eyes and find out if there is any difference with your eyes open or closed. And then notice that the tendency will be to come back up into the mind to think about it. What if you notice whatever mental tendency arises, and then let it sink back down.

- If you have a hard time getting out of the mental body, you can begin with a trance induction. From there you can elicit a memory, and use that to go through.
- If you continually avoid going all the way through, continually looping back up into thoughts or surface emotions, there is still some identification and attachment to the story. This may be a signal to go back in time to where the story began and do a "change history", or "ally from the future."
- Be aware of ego shelves; landings in the physical, mental or emotional bodies which are relatively comfortable or peaceful. Find out if it has a bottom. If there is a bottom, this is a shelf. Or you may find there is a feeling of sleepiness, and you would rather sleep than keep going. This is also a shelf. Discover what is under that.
- You can also drop directly into essence. You do not have to go through all these layers; you can go right from anger into essence; you can go right from hurt into essence. But if you skip steps that are unfinished, then these are latent tendencies. These are what is called "vasanas." They are going to await the right moment to be experienced.

The truth is you only have to do it once and discover the truth of who you are and then never come back from that. It only needs to be done once, otherwise it may become another technique which you may or may not want – as a technique it is fine, but that is like settling for the crumbs.

The Passion of the Fixation

Dyad:
- Identify the passion of the fixation which has been running this life.
- Ask the repeating question:

    How does (the passion: anger, pride, doubt etc.) show up?

- Pick one example of how the passion shows up in your life.
- What triggers it? How does it begin? What are the submodalities?
- <u>Anchor</u>
- <u>Fire the anchor</u>, and trace the kinesthetics back to the earliest similar experience you can remember.

- Drop through the nesting of emotions.
- Future pace: imagine a situation in the future where the passion might have a tendency to arise. Without suppressing it or acting it out, directly experience whatever is present.

The Imitation of Essence

Dyad:

- Identify the quality of Essence imitated or avoided by the character fixation of this body.

  Ask the repeating question:

  How in your life have you imitated or avoided this quality of Essence?

- Pick a specific example.
- How does it begin? What are the submodalities?
- Anchor
- Fire the anchor, and trace back to earliest memory of imitation.

  Drop through the nesting of emotions.

- Future pace.

Pride and Worthlessness

Dyad:

This exercise examines the "I am somebody trance" and the " I am nobody" trance. Both are forms of arrogance.

- Remember a time when pride was present.
- Find the trigger and submodalities.
- <u>Anchor</u> the pride.

- Remember a time when you were little when pride first showed up.
- Fully associate with the memory.
- <u>Anchor,</u> using same as above.

- Find a neutral state.

- Remember a time you felt worthless.
- Find the trigger and submodalities.
- <u>Anchor</u> the worthlessness.

- Remember an early memory, perhaps when you first felt worthless.
- Fully associate with the memory.
- <u>Anchor</u> using same as previous.

- Remember a time you either felt special or worthless.
- <u>Collapse anchors.</u>
- Allow dissolving of all form.

- Future pace: "In the future whenever you feel pride or worthlessness, what if you experience it without moving …"

Independence and Dependence

Dyad:

Both are styles of control. Each has the other behind it.

- Remember a scene in which you felt dependent.
- "Teach me how to do it?" (what are the submodalities?)
- <u>Anchor</u>

- Remember a scene in which you were independent.
- Teach me how to do it? (submodalities?)
- <u>Anchor</u>

- <u>Collapse anchors</u>

The Puritan and the Hedonist

Dyad:
- Go to a time where the judge or puritan manifested.
- What is the structure of it? (submodalities?)
- Find the positive intention.
- Anchor

- Go to a time when you were a hedonist or in rebellion.
- What is the structure of it? (submodalities?)
- Find the positive intention.
- Anchor

- Go back to a time when one or the other started.
- Collapse anchors.

Shame and Pride

Dyad:

- Shame and pride go together. One or the other may be more on the surface of the fixation, while the other may be more hidden.
- Ask the repeating question:

  What do you feel ashamed about?

- Then pick one thing you feel ashamed about.
- Where does it start?
- What are the submodalities? (physical, mental, emotional)
- What is the positive intention of the shame?
- <u>Anchor</u>

- Ask the repeating question:

  What are you proud of?

- Pick one thing you are proud about.
- How does it start?
- What are the submodalities?
- What is the positive intention of the pride?
- <u>Anchor</u>

- <u>Collapse anchors</u>
- Or, go back to a time when one or the other started, <u>Collapse anchors.</u>

Loyalty and Betrayal

The Center of the Circle:

- What if the center of a circle represented the experience of being true to your Self, the Beloved. Imagine standing in the center and find the submodalities of being true to your Self.
- Imagine walking away from the center point in the circle. What does the betrayal feel like? What are the submodalities?
- Turn in to the center and notice what has to happen.

False loyalty:

- Find out where loyalty has been misplaced; ask the repeating question:

  Who or what have you been loyal to, at the cost of being true to your Self?

- What is the positive intention of this betrayal in the name of loyalty?
- Find the submodalities of one memory where you were "loyal" at the expense of your own Self.
- Anchor

- Find the submodalities of a memory when you were being true to your Self (desired state).
- Anchor

- Go to an early memory of being loyal to someone or something other than your Self
- Collapse anchors

Betrayal:
- Remember a time when you felt betrayed.
- Find the submodalities?
- <u>Anchor.</u>

- Remember a time when you betrayed your Self or another?
- What are the submodalities of this experience?
- <u>Anchor.</u>

- What was the positive intention behind your actions?
- Go to an early memory where you felt betrayed.
- <u>Collapse Anchors.</u>

The Judge or Super-ego

Dyad:

- Remember a memory when you were judging yourself about something you did, or something you "should have done."
- What is the trigger, and the submodalities of the reaction?
- Anchor

- What is the positive intention of the judge?
- Remember another time when you did not judge yourself.
- What are the submodalities?
- Anchor
- Remember the first memory, collapse anchors

Love

Dyads:
- What is it like when you need love?
- What are the submodalities?

- What is it like falling in love?
- What are the submodalities?

- What is it like to BE love?
- What are the submodalities?

Notes:

Needing love: Feeling that someone else should be loving you the way you want them to; frequently accompanied by hurt and anger; a belief that

" I deserve"; a belief that I am a separate entity and my agenda and needs are important.

Falling in love: Fixated on an outside object. A feeling of love mixed with desire and hormones. "I want that for me". Hormonal, adrenaline. Fever or narcotic that kills the pain.

Being Love: The recognition that love is who you are. Much deeper than than the body or the emotions. In this love which is one Self, the body, the mind and the emotions can relax. Love is recognized everywhere.

Lust: Freeing the Jailer
(Passion for excess)

Dyads:

- Ask the repeating question:

  Where in your life do you turn away from the truth
  in the name of lust or passion?

- Select a particular time you experienced lust (sexual, food, wind surfing, etc)
- What are the submodalities?
- Anchor

- Remember a similar circumstance without lust (desired state)
- Find the submodalities.
- Anchor

- Go back to this first experience of lust and collapse anchors.
- Bring the desired state into the original experience of lust.

- Future pace: Imagine a relevant time in the future when you may be tempted to act with lust. Fire the desired state anchor.

Projection

"Projection" is an unconscious mental process of imagining something happening in an "other", rather than happening in oneself. It is imagining that it is happening over "there", rather than "here."

It begins with Consciousness identifying itself as an idealized image of a separate ego. Aspects of thought, feeling and behavior which do not fit the idealized image, are ignored, denied, dissociated. These aspects are considered "not me."

The circumstances and people in one's life become the screen on which these denied aspects of consciousness get projected. For instance, if the aspect of greed is denied and ignored in oneself, it will be projected onto someone "other" in the movie of one's life circumstances. "He is greedy, (I am not greedy)."

Both positive and negative aspects may be denied as being within oneself, and then get projected outward onto the screen of one's "Situational body."

The circumstances, and people in your life, are a reflection of your own mind.

This reflection mercifully shows you where you are attached to being something in particular, rather than to the totality itself. It mercifully shows you where you are avoiding or hiding from all of that which you truly are. With right understanding, projection can be one of the signs pointing home.

When you are awake to the truth of your Self, you see Love everywhere, you see your Self everywhere, and there is nothing "other" to project upon. All is your own Self.

Exercise: The Root of Projection:

1. Begin with a trance induction.
2. Identify a time when you were "projecting" onto someone in your life.

3. Watch the memory like a movie, seeing it with "new eyes."
4. Watching the movie again, notice something you may not have before.
5. Replace the person with one of your parents, then watch the same movie,
6. Replace your parent with an image of yourself, and watch the same movie.
7. Allow whatever insight has happened to deepen, as you allow the screen of the mind to be empty, and rest deeper inside your Self.
8. After the session take a moment to share what you have realized.

APPENDIX

First International Enneagram
Conference

Stanford University August,1994

I have never met anyone who doesn't want to be happy. The desire for happiness is the bottom line for the human species and maybe for all species. Everyone wants to be happy. The question is: how is it possible that this desire for happiness is threatening to destroy our species and Mother Earth. How is it possible? This is really a burning question that I have had. And I know that many of us have had this question: How is it possible that the desire for happiness creates suffering? What I have discovered is that it is possible to end suffering. I have come here to share with you the great good news that the end of suffering is waking up from the trance induction of who you think you are.

The exquisiteness of the Enneagram is that it gives us the structure of who you are not. The great tragedy that I see in the use of the Enneagram is that people use it to go further to sleep - to say, "I'm a six and you're a four and that's why we are acting this way." Or "who are you? ... you're an eight, then you must be .... " This is going deeper to sleep, rather than using the fixation to recognize that it is a trance induction. It is, in fact, not who you are. When you recognize that it is not who you are, then there is a willingness and a possibility to wake up and discover who you really are.

In the past this has been very rare. Back through recorded history, how many awake, enlightened beings do we find? Maybe one in a generation. Maybe one in ten generations. But that is no longer acceptable. It can not be just one, some where, some time. As Mother Earth is dying, she is casting the seeds to the wind. The possibility now is for you, personally, directly, to recognize that you are the Buddha, you are the Christ, you are the second coming. And the only thing that stands in the way of your direct realization of That, is the belief that you are a fixation. This results in justifications to continue the patterns of suffering, and an acting out of the subconscious identification with the fixation.

I suspect that for everyone reading this book there have been moments when your mind was quiet, there were no thoughts, and you were not paying attention to your body sensations. There may have been a moment when you discovered something beyond words, beyond time and space and beyond the idea of "me and my story." That moment exposes the truth of existence and the truth of who you are.

The possibility is living your life from the depths of that revelation. The only obscuration to the fulfillment of that revelation is the subconscious identification as a body, which has certain desires and needs and a certain past and future. The obscuration is the belief that this body is "me." In that moment when your mind was quiet, there was no "me," yet something was still there. It is That which never changes, does not come and go. It was there before you were born and there after you die, and It is there every moment in between. Yet It is so familiar, that It gets overlooked. It gets overlooked in this identification and belief that I am some body.

This is the great gift of the Enneagram. When used correctly, it uncovers the subconscious identification that "I am some body." What I would like to do here today, first of all, is redefine the Enneagram in terms of the way that it is known. I learned it as the "Enneagram of Personality," and I believe that everyone at this conference uses it as the Enneagram of Personality. But in fact, that is not accurate in my experience. It is not the Enneagram of Personality. It is the Enneagram of Character Fixation. There is a distinct difference.

I would like to present a model of the psyche that illustrates where Character Fixation lies, relative to the Personality and Essence. I find this model to be simple, and immediately useful. The outermost ring is personality; this is the surface level, the most superficial. When most people go to therapy, they go to therapy to change their personality: to stop smoking, to lose weight, to have a better relationship, to have less fear and more confidence. All of those are personality changes. That is a step. Everyone in this room has had some kind of therapy. It is the religion of our time. You do not go to a priest and confess. You go to a therapist. So, in therapy, you may have discovered that you can change your personality. You can be more confident. You can stop smoking. You can break certain habits and patterns. But even in changing your personality, it does not touch what is deeper. And what is deeper - what the personality is built on - is the Character Fixation. This is what the Enneagram describes.

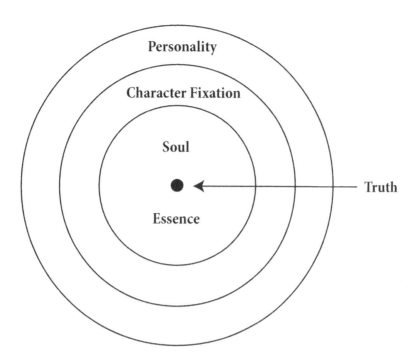

You will find very different personalities with the same Character Fixation. The personality fundamentally, ultimately, is not the problem. Working on the level of personality or ego strengthening, can be very valuable at a certain stage, but ultimately it is not satisfying. You want something deeper. You are not satisfied with just a better personality or a better life.

In this dream, in this trance induction of me and my story, most New Age therapies are set up to give you a better story. You <u>can</u> change your story. If you have a negative internal dialogue going on, it is definitely better to have a positive internal dialogue. At a certain stage, changing your story can be valuable. It can be important to know that you are not stuck in that particular story. However, ultimately that is not satisfying.

You get more money, you get a better job, you have a better relationship, but always "you" show up. That is the fly in the ointment! So you can have a better life, I am not against it. But if you stop there, you are selling yourself short.

What I notice is that people who reach a certain level of a better life, then tend to recycle. They start going back into the same old issues, finding out whose fault and why, and what happened with my parents. Finally, that gets to be such an old story, that you are ready to finish it. That is the good news - that the Enneagram presents the possibility for finishing it.

• • •

In my experience of training therapists over the years, what I have discovered is that the basis of good therapy is not how deep the client can go, it is how deep the therapist is. Another gift of the Enneagram is that it gives us a structure which points to the depth of Being. I have discovered a model for being a successful therapist: to be Awareness, Emptiness and Love.

This structure is also the base bones that the Enneagram is built upon.

Awareness, Emptiness and Love represent the three bodies of manifestation. This is a very important distinction - to recognize that there is a physical, emotional and mental body. Ideally the physical body and the senses are in awareness. Awareness without a story, without judgment, without a personal goal or personal need - just pure awareness.

In the mental body, the mind is quiet, silent and empty - without having to know - without having to be right - without having to do anything. What I have discovered is that the depth is revealed in "not knowing." This "not knowing" I call "emptiness," "silence," "quiet mind." All of our society is built on knowing: "If I just know enough, then I'll know the right thing to do and then I will get the rewards. If I know enough, I will be successful." The challenge here is to be willing to not know, to allow the mind to be quiet.

In this quiet, naturally there is an open heart. This open heart is love itself. In this there is the possibility for actually being of service.

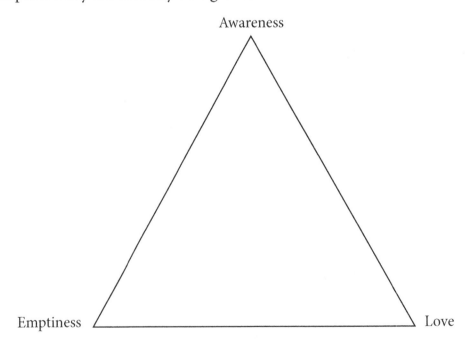

This is a model that I was working with for a number of years before I met my teacher, Sri Poonjaji. In 1990 when I met my teacher, I had an enormous discovery - that in Sanskrit, the word for "True Self" is Satchitananda. The amazing revelation is that the meaning of Satchitananda corresponds exactly with Awareness, Emptiness and Love.

Sat means Consciousness as "Being", Chit means Consciousness as "Intelligence", and Ananda means Consciousness as "Love and Bliss." In Sanskrit, these three qualities are within one word, because in reality they cannot be divided, just as you cannot separate the heat, the light, and the burning out of fire.

But for the model of the Enneagram, we are making believe that we can make this distinction. Awareness, Emptiness and Love are three qualities of the True Self which in reality are inseparable. This is Satchitananda. This is the Self.

What if every time you say anything referring to "myself" or every time you say "I," you refer to this Self. What if "I" refers to limitless, immortal, conscious love? What if what you are referring to has nothing to do with this body?

• • •

I believe that most people are all already in trance and the possibility is to wake up from the trance. The trance induction starts with the physical material universe - believing that it is solid, discrete and real. Yet we already know from science - from Heisenberg and Quantum physics, that the physical universe is an illusion. It is not the way it appears.

It appears that there are separate, discrete objects in space, but scientists say that if you look at it closely enough you will find the "atom," and when you look at an atom closely enough, you find that it is mainly empty space, In that space, smaller than the atom, one finds, "protons", "neutrons" "electrons." But when you again look closely enough, what you find is either a particle or a wave, depending upon your point of view. And it is blinking on and off!

So with just a slight shift in the spectral field of your eye, what we are calling discrete, separate objects in the material universe can be seen as a standing wave form, blinking on and off. It is a trance induction. It is in illusion, a magic trick. It doesn't really exist.

Within this universal trance, there is a trance induction of the human being, believing that "human" is where beingness resides. In the word itself, "human being" implies that that is where being is. What about when the body disappears? Does that mean being disappears? The possibility is to discover that who you are is immortal being - present before and after the body. But this can't be discovered as long as you believe you are a number or a type. The possibility is to wake up from the trance induction of the fixation.

The Enneagram is the western gift to the enlightenment process. In the past, as I said, maybe one soul every who knows how many years wakes up. But now the potential is there for everyone and the Enneagram gives you the owner's manual so you can discover you are not the machinery.

The western myth, as far as I see, starts with Adam and Eve. When Adam and Eve are in the garden, they are happy, they are at one, there is no self consciousness, there is a flowing with things. But they are not Self Realized. Then the devil shows up.

What does the devil do? He says, "O.k., eat from the fruit of the tree of knowledge of good and evil." What is this? This is the mind. The mind is the duality of good and evil, right and wrong, on and off. In eating the fruit of the tree of knowledge of good and evil, suddenly there is self-consciousness. There is shame. In this moment of shame, they are out of the garden. And in being out of the garden, their seed populates the earth and destroys it. The mind, which has rebelled against God, is running wild as the ruler. With the mind running wild as the ruler, we have ignorance, poverty, mayhem, greed, selfishness, ecological devastation. Finally the mind has to come back to its rightful place. It has to give up this seat as the ruler, to God.

We can think of this metaphorically as a deal with the devil. This comes up a lot in our culture. The devil will make a deal with you. He will give you anything you want - basically that means money, sex and power. The only thing the devil wants in exchange is your soul, and you won't miss it any way, you didn't even know you had one.

What is this deal? Why is it that the devil can give you the objects of pleasure (money, sex and power), and why does he need your soul? The joke is that the devil needs your soul because the objects of pleasure are only desirable if the light of the soul is shining on them, is turned towards them.

It is like sitting in the movies. As long as you are watching the screen, watching the colored lights flickering on and off, you can have the experience of feeling sad and crying, or feeling afraid or angry. In the fascination with the movie, there is never a turning away to see the light. If you are willing to turn away from the movie, you find out that it is just light and the movie disappears.

What I have discovered is that most people don't want the movie to disappear and therefore are not really interested in turning towards the light. Unless the light appears as another object in the movie. "I want to take this piece with me. This piece is pretty good. I have got my job. I have got my Mercedes. Let's take that and turn towards the light." But since it is impossible to be both watching the movie and turning towards the light, "the light" becomes another object in the movie to be captured by mind. Once captured it becomes, "my light, my truth."

Ultimately, finally, you find out that the objects of pleasure do not leave you satisfied. They leave a bitterness. They leave an aftertaste of suffering. It may be pleasurable in the moment. But finally, they are not satisfying. At that point, you are willing to turn away from the movie and turn towards the source, turn towards the light.

What the Enneagram does is that it gives us the characters of the movie in beautiful detail.

• • •

These are the qualities of Essence that I have discovered show up at each of the points of fixation. You could say that each fixation is masking a quality of Essence. What I have found is when the fixation is not there these qualities of Essence show up.

Qualities of Essence

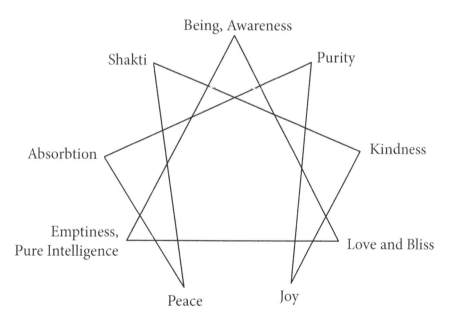

What shines through a fully aware, fully mature, real human being is: awareness, purity, kindness, love, joy, peace, emptiness, absorption and Shakti or power. What I would like you to notice about these is that they are still clustered around

Satchitananda, Point Nine is beingness, which is what awareness is, and Shakti and purity are qualities of being.

Pure Intelligence or Emptiness is at point Six, and peace and absorption are qualities of emptiness.

Love is at point Three on the Enneagram, and kindness and joy are flurescenses or qualities of Love. These qualities which show up - kindness and joy around Love - are qualities of the soul - qualities of the subtle body.

These qualities of the subtle body or the soul get developed over lifetimes of tests. You can meet people who have a certain essence that is obvious and shining. They may not be awake, they may not be Self Realized, but the Essence is clear and obvious.

I worked with an American Indian elder a number of years ago, doing sweat lodges. Anyone who met this man would see this face of goodness, essential kindness, that was transcendent of any fixation. The veiling of the fixation would be there or it would disappear, but the essential kindness wouldn't leave.

These qualities of essence, basic goodness, are qualities of the soul. This is the possibility - the true human potential.

Essence is what is veiled once the movie starts rolling. Once I am "some body", then you will find there is a quality of fixation that is either imitating or moving away from each of these qualities of Essence. Once "I am some body" shows up, then there is a physical body, a mental body and an emotional body - sensations, thoughts and feelings. This is generally what people are referring to when they say "me" or "myself." The physical, emotional and mental body, "that is who I am. " That is the trance induction.

One of the natural consequences of that trance induction is anger. Because if who I am is a physical body, there is anger about who is in control. If I am a physical body, there is fear and doubt about the survival of this body. If I am a physical body and I am angry and I am afraid, now I also have needs. I need love. And so deceit and neediness appear. Deceit is a mask to fool the desired object in an attempt to get an idea of love.

Now instead of Awareness, what shows up is anger. Instead of Emptiness and Intelligence, what shows up is fear and doubt - or thinking, which is the imitation of True Intelligence. True intelligence is Silent and Empty. The inner dialogue, the trance induction of the commentator, keeps you in the trance that "this is me, this is my story, this is my past and these are my experiences." And once you have this commentator, there appears to be a "doer." I imagine myself to be doing something, and to be either doing it right and good, or to be doing it wrong. And instead of Pure and Immortal Love and Bliss, what shows up is a search for Love, a neediness, and the creation of an image that one believes will get them what they think is Love.

Once you know the fixations, you can't fool yourself any more. You can't kid yourself into thinking that this is just what is spontaneously arising. Because you know the difference between spontaneity and fixation. It is obvious. It is apparent.

The Enneagram starts from the belief that I am somebody and since I am some body, I am angry, afraid and needy. That is the human condition. Then, not only am I some body, I am a lustful, lazy, angry, prideful, deceitful, envious, avaricious, doubtful, glutton! Then - people want to be a better one of those. That's the joke.

You find that you can in fact become a better one, but still there is something missing, some basic fundamental gnawing. There is something that is not satisfied - if you are lucky. Only if you are lucky. This is called spiritual ripeness. For most people in the world - all they can think about is the next meal. And if they can get the next meal together, then shelter for their family, or clothing. This is what most people in the world have to concern themselves with.

We reading this book are the privileged of the world. We are the princes and princesses - the kings and queens of this world. We have enough time and enough money to sit and read and reflect. This makes you one of the privileged elite, and gives you the possibility to wake up and finally finish the story of suffering. Or you can choose to recycle back into the insecurity of "but who is going to pay the rent?" and, " but what about my job", and you are back at the level of the poor souls who do not have enough to eat. But this is a lie. You are betraying this gift that has been given to you. You are betraying the potential of this lifetime.

Powers in Sanskrit are called "siddhis." It took lifetimes of merit to acquire these siddhis. So now you have the power to fly around the world - you can come and sit here and not worry about your next meal. You have the choice to use this power wisely. If you use it wisely, then you didn't take anything from all the ones who are starving, you have given them a gift. Then your life is not an extra burden on Mother Earth. It is a giving back to Mother Earth.

Everyone would love to stop the starvation, but how many meals can you give to the people starving right now? Not very many. But a quiet mind you can give to anyone. And the ending of fixation you can transmit to everyone in this hall. That is a gift that you can actually pass on. Then this life is meaningful, worthwhile. Then Mother Earth celebrates you. Then you do not have to worry about your existence. Mother Earth takes care of your existence. You do not have to worry about who is going to pay the rent. Mother Earth takes care of it. If it is meant to be paid you will pay it. And if it is not, you won't.

• • •

The desire for happiness that is alive in every human being generally gets translated into more, better and different. More food, better food, different food. More sex, better sex, different sex. More stuff, better stuff, different stuff. You go through lifetimes of acquiring and accumulating more, better and different, until finally you notice it is not satisfying. You want something deeper. This is spiritual maturity. This is spiritual ripeness.

If you can hear what I am saying and it makes sense to you, then this is you. Most people would have no idea what I am talking about. If this makes sense to you, this means you are spiritually ripe - you're ready - you understand this. Then take the challenge of your lifetime. It takes the willingness to go against all the conditioning. It takes the willingness for a jail break.

Earth is a slave planet. Everyone is asleep, and everyone stays asleep because we get enough to eat, and enough goodies, "maybe I am in jail, but hey, I've got wall to wall carpet, a color TV. . . . It's not so bad."

When the desire for happiness comes out through the fixation, it shows up as one of the passions. The desire for happiness in the Eight shows up as lust. The desire for happiness in a Two shows up as pride. Desire for happiness in a Three shows up as deceit.

The passion is the capturing of the desire for happiness by the mind, filtering it through the fixation. The antidote is what is also called the path. It is the willingness to not act out and not repress the rising of fixation. This is the possibility. We came from 1950's repressed culture. As a counterculture we have all, to varying degrees, acted out. Many of us have acted out sex or rage in the name of freedom. In a variety of ways we have acted out our fixation and justified it. The challenge of this lifetime is to be willing to stop the fixation. Finally, ultimately, to neither act it out nor repress it.

This is new territory. If you neither act it out nor repress it, there's an enormous burning. This burning is the funeral pyre of fixation. You can give everything to this fire, throw everything that can be burned into the fire. Then discover what can not be burned. Discover what is left.

This burning is the flame of freedom. It can not be captured. It can not be extinguished. It can not be bought or sold. The ripe souls are the ones that are hungry for it. The ones that are longing for something deeper. In this longing for something deeper, there is the possibility to not being willing to play the game of the fixation any more.

•   •   •

Holy ideas are good news and bad news. The bad news is that each fixation takes the holy idea and incorporates it as a way of justifying the fixation. For Nine, the holy idea is love. The Nine says, "I want to be a loving person. I want you to love me. I want to be lovable. Therefore, instead of getting angry, I will go to sleep." This is how the holy idea now becomes a justification for perpetuating suffering.

The holy idea for the One is perfection. The One internalizes this holy idea of desired perfection and uses it to create the judge of what is imperfect - judging myself for being imperfect - judging you for being imperfect - judging the world for being imperfect. All in the name of the holy idea of perfection.

For the Two the holy idea is freedom. The two internalizes this to say, "I am free to serve you. I like taking care of you." Again, this holy idea gets captured by the mind and is used to perpetuate suffering.

For the Eight the holy idea is truth. In the name of truth, Eights are the biggest liars and bullies on the Enneagram. Because "I know the truth and you don't. Let me tell you what is wrong with you." Now what happens is that truth becomes personalized, as if it is my truth versus your truth. This is the suffering. There is no my truth versus your truth. That is just trance induction versus trance induction, dream versus dream.

Each of these fixations internalize the holy idea and use it as a way to continue it. The possibility is for the holy idea to be something that is ego transcendent. Since you are starting with an ego, which is a trance induction of the mind, it is the mind that has to start to search for its own freedom. The mind wants to grasp on to something that seems tangible and real, so the mind grasps on to an internalized object - or a holy idea of truth, freedom, love … And when you desire this more than anything else. When you desire truth or love or freedom or source - more than anything else - if you are willing to give your life for it, then this holy idea becomes transcendent of ego. Transcendent of personal life. It leads you to what is deeper.

The possibility is discovering the depths. Most people live on the surface. By the surface, I mean thoughts of me and my story and the feelings of anger and hurt about who did what to whom. This is all a way of avoiding the depths of terror and despair. But, I have discovered that the trap door which leads into the depths is underneath the despair and the terror.

True joy and happiness are transcendent of the Enneagram. The Enneagram deals with the negative emotions, and what we have discovered is that these negative emotions are limited. For most fixations, the most surface, most easily experienced emotion is anger. If you add in a story, you get the variations of anger such as irritation, frustration, vengeance and jealousy. Most people can feel irritated a dozen times in a day and don't think anything of it. Anger is socially acceptable. I can either be angry at myself because I did it, or I can be angry at you because you did it. That is living in the story of the surface emotion.

What you will find is that if you are willing to go deeper, under anger, almost always you are going to find hurt or sadness. Hurt or sadness is being defended by anger. But if you don't act the anger out and if you don't repress it - and the Enneagram is all about styles of acting out and repression - if you do neither one of these, you can experience the anger without a story and go deeper.

In going deeper, you will almost always find hurt and sadness. This is where most of the population lives most of the time. If they are in their emotions they are either hurt about something or they are angry about something. For some people it is easier to express the anger, and for some it is easier to express the hurt, but they bounce back and forth between these two.

The tendency then is to stop there, to say, " I am hurt and I am sad and it is because of you … it is because of my parents … if only I had a different childhood …" Now, in making this mental story you have dissociated yourself from the emotion. Now you are not even feeling the anger and the sadness, you are in your ideas. That is a way of dissociating.

But, if you don't go in to the story - which is the fixation - and you don't repress it and you don't act it out, you go deeper. Underneath you will almost always find fear. Most people don't want to feel fear. Fear is undesirable. Fear means there is something wrong with me. Fear means I'm not adequate. Fear means I am a coward. Fear means I don't know the right thing to do.

All these are trance inductions about what fear means. So as soon as most people get even close to feeling fear, they pop back out and start to feel anger and sadness or tell themselves a story.

The possibility is to cut the story, to cut the trance induction of the past and the future, and to allow yourself to drown in fear. This is very rare. No one may have ever told you to do this before. The therapists usually tell you how to move away from fear - how to suppress it or how to change it into courage. But if you actually sink in and you really experience it, you will find that under fear is despair - and that is the good news!

All the ego structures are set up to never feel despair. All therapy is set up to move you away from despair. All the workshops are set up so you feel empowered and you can create your reality and you don't have to feel despair. However, despair is at the root of every ego fixation. The truth of the situation is the ego isn't good enough! It isn't going to make it. It doesn't exist!

The possibility is to actually head towards what you are most afraid of - to head towards what all the conditioning says move away from. This is the trap door. It is the escape hatch. The way out of the fixation and the story is to invite despair. To be willing to face the unbearableness of despair - that you are hopeless, helpless, not good enough. That you don't know, you are never going to get it, and you are going to be left alone. So you call it out and you experience it. Without suppressing it. Without acting it out. Then you sink in and you find what is deeper.

And what is deeper? Most people report that there is nothing there. But this "nothing there" is not true emptiness, it is a mental emptiness. It is a dead flat emptiness, which I call a black hole. This is what gets avoided at all costs. "I don't want to fall into a black hole, I won't exist! I won't come out alive." This is true. The ego can't exist there, it won't come out alive from there. But you are not an ego, you are immortal Intelligence which has gone into an imaginary sleep, pretending to be an ego.

The French existentialists, Sartre and Camus, found the black hole, but that is as far as they went, they didn't go through it.

Fours and Fives live on the edge of this black hole, as a fixation style. Fours and Fives feel the wounding of the black hole, that there is something missing, that there should be something there.

This inner black hole is remarkably similar to the black hole in outer space, which scientists believe, literally sucks the event horizon of time and space into itself, The

Four tries to avoid the black hole through emotions, "If I have enough emotions, that will fill it." Fives try to avoid it with information. "If I just know enough, it will save me from the black hole." Most other fixations are more asleep to it. Most don't even know it is there. But this is what is waiting under despair.

The FOUR GATEKEEPERS ~ EXCERPT *from the* YOGA VASHASISTRA

"**R**ama, the highest form of dispassion born of pure discrimination has arisen in your heart. As long as this highest wisdom does not dawn in the heart, the person revolves endlessly in this wheel of birth and death. Pray listen to my exposition of this wisdom with a concentrated mind.

This wisdom destroys the forest of ignorance. Roaming in this forest one undergoes confusion and seemingly interminable suffering. One should therefore approach an enlightened teacher and by asking the right question, with the right attitude elicit the teaching.

It then becomes an integral part of one's being. The fool asks irrelevant questions irreverently, and the greater fool is he who spurns the sages' wisdom. Oh Rama, you are indeed among the best among seekers for you have duly reflected on the truth and you are inspired by the best form of dispassion, and I am sure that what I am going to say to you will find a firm seat in your heart. Indeed one should positively strive to enthrone wisdom in one's heart for the mind is unsteady like a monkey. And one should then avoid unwise company.

Rama, there are four gatekeepers at the entrance to the realm of freedom. They are self control, spirit of inquiry, contentment, and good company. The wise seeker should diligently cultivate these friendships with a pure heart and receptive mind.

Without the veil of doubt or the restlessness of the mind listen to this exposition of the nature and means of liberation, Oh Rama. For not until the Supreme Being is realized will the dreadful misery of birth and death come to an end. If this deadly serpent known as ignorant life is not overcome here and now, it gives rise to interminable suffering not only in this, but in countless lifetimes to come. One cannot ignore this suffering, one should overcome it by the means of the wisdom that I shall impart to you.

Oh Rama, if you thus overcome this sorrow of repetitive history called samsara you will live here on earth itself like a God, like Brahma or Vishnu. For when delusion is gone and truth is realized by means of inquiry into your own self nature, when the mind is at peace, when the heart leaps to the supreme truth, when all the disturbing thought waves in the mind stuff have subsided and there is an unbroken flow of peace and the heart is filled with the bliss of the absolute, when thus the truth has been seen in the heart, then this very world itself becomes an abode of bliss.

Such a person has nothing to acquire nor nothing to shun. He is untainted by the defects of life, untouched by its sorrow, he does not come into being or go out, though he appears to come and go in the eye of the beholder. Even religious duties are not found to be necessary. He is not affected by the past tendencies which have lost their momentum, His mind has given up its restlessness and he rests in the bliss that is his essential nature.

Such bliss is possible only by self knowledge, not by any other means. Hence one should apply oneself constantly to self knowledge; this alone is one's duty. In order to cross this formidable ocean of samsara of the suffering of repetitive history, one should resort to that which is eternal and unchanging. He alone is the best among men, oh Rama, whose mind rests in the eternal and is therefore fully self–controlled and at peace.

Inquiry which is the second gate–keeper to liberation should be undertaken by an intelligence that has been purified by a close study of the truth and this inquiry should be unbroken. By such inquiry the intelligence becomes sharp and is able to realize the supreme. Hence inquiry alone is the best remedy for the long lasting illness known as samsara.

The eternal is not attained by rights or by rituals or by pilgrimages or by wealth. It is only to be attained by the conquest of one's own mind, by the cultivation of wisdom. Hence gods, demons, demi–gods, or men, everyone should constantly seek the conquest of the mind and self control which are the fruits of wisdom.

When the mind is at peace, pure, tranquil, free from delusion or hallucination, untangled and free from cravings, it does not long for anything and it does not reject anything. This is self-control or conquest of the mind, one of the four gate–keepers that I have mentioned.

All that is good and auspicious flows from self–control; all evil is dispelled by self-control. No gain and no pleasure in this world or in heaven is comparable to the delight of self–control; even the food you eat tastes better.

Whoever wears the armor of self-control is not harmed by sorrow. So inquiry which is the next gate–keeper should be undertaken by a purified intelligence. The wise person regards strength, intellect, efficiency and timely action all as the fruits of inquiry. Indeed kingdom, prosperity, enjoyment as well as final liberation are all the fruits of inquiry.

The spirit of inquiry protects one from the calamities that befall the unthinking fool. When the mind has been rendered dull by the absence of inquiry, even the cool rays of the moon turn into deadly weapons and the childish imagination throws up a goblin in every dark spot. Hence the non–inquiring fool is really a storehouse of sorrow.

It is the absence of inquiry that gives rise to actions that are harmful to oneself and to others, and to numerous psychosomatic illnesses. Therefore one should avoid the company of such unthinking people. They in whom the spirit of inquiry is ever awake illumine the world, enlighten all who come in contact with them, dispel the ghosts created by an ignorant mind and realize the falsity of sense pleasures and their objects.

Oh, Rama, in the light of inquiry there is realization of the eternal and unchanging reality; this is the supreme. With it one does not long for any other gain nor does one spurn anything. He is free from delusion and attachment. He is not inactive nor does he get drowned in action. He lives and functions in this world and at the end of a natural life span he reaches the blissful state of total freedom.

The "I" of spiritual inquiry does not lose its sight even in the midst of all activities. Whoever does not have this "I" is indeed to be pitied. It is better to be born as a frog in the mud, or a worm in dung, or a snake in a hole than one without this "I".

And what is inquiry? Inquiry is to inquire, "Who Am I?" How has this evil of repetitive history come into being? This is true inquiry. Knowledge of truth arises from such inquiry, from such knowledge there follows tranquility in oneself, and then there arises the supreme peace that surpasses all understanding and is the end of all sorrow.

He who has quaffed the nectar of contentment does not relish craving for sense pleasures. No delight in this world is as sweet as contentment which destroys all sins. What is contentment? To renounce all cravings for what is not obtained unsought and to be satisfied with what comes unsought without being elated or depressed, this is contentment.

As long as one is not satisfied in the Self he will be subject to sorrow. With the rise of contentment the heart blossoms. The contented man who possesses nothing owns the world.

Satsang, or the company of wise, and enlightened people, is yet another gate-keeper to liberation. Satsang enlarges one's intelligence, destroys one's ignorance and one's psychological distress. Whatever may be the cost, however difficult it may be, whatever obstacles may stand in the way, Satsang should never be neglected. For Satsang alone is one's light on the path of life. Satsang is, indeed, superior to all other forms of practice, and one should by every means find it.

These four: contentment, Satsang, the company of the wise, the spirit of inquiry, and self–control, are the four surest means by which they who are drowning in this ocean of Samsara can be saved. Contentment is the supreme gain. Satsang is the best companion. The spirit of inquiry is the greatest wisdom and self–control is supreme happiness.

Whoever is endowed with the qualities I have enumerated thus far is qualified to listen to what I am about to reveal, and you are, indeed, such a qualified person, Oh, Rama, only he who wishes to hear this is ripe for liberation. "

Glossary

Analog marking Emphasizing a part of a sentence using nonverbals; e.g. a louder tone, an eye movement, a hand gesture, etc.

Ananda Pure conceptionless Bliss.

Anchor The process by which any representation (internal or external) gets connected to and triggers a subsequent string of responses.

Associated Being in an experience or memory as fully and completely as possible with all the senses.

Auditory The sense of hearing.

Behavior Activity humans engage in such as thinking, eye movements, breathing changes, gestures and so forth.

Behavioral Flexibility The ability to vary one's behavior in order to elicit a desired response from another person.

Bodhisattva One whose life is dedicated to the enlightenment of all Being.

Chunk Size The size of object, situation or experience being considered. This can be altered by chunking up to a more general category, chunking down to a more specific category, or chunking laterally to others of the same type or class.

Communication The process of conveying information by language, signs, symbols, and behavior. It can be directionalized, which is to say that the place you end a conversation is different from where it began. As in effective therapy it moves toward an desired outcome.

Congruent When all of a person's internal strategies, behaviors and parts are in agreement and working together coherently.

Context The surrounding within which a communication or response occurs. The context is one of the cues that elicit specific responses.

Context reframing Placing a problem response or behavior in a different context that gives it a new and different meaning (usually more positive).

Cross-over Mirroring Matching a person, but with a different type of behavior; e.g. pacing breathing with hand movements.

Dharma Truth/path.

Dissociated Experiencing an event or memory from any perspective other than seeing out of our own eyes. This can be a limiting process when it prevents positive resources and experiences from being fully experienced. It can also be used skillfully in the therapeutic context, to view highly emotional or traumatic memories from a resourceful state, allowing for the possibility of learning and insight.

Ecology Considering the effects of a change on the large system instead of on just one isolated behavior, part, or person. A concern for the totality or pattern of relationships between a being and its environment. In reference to internal ecology, it means the pattern of values, strategies, and behaviors one embodies in relationship to himself.

Elicitation Determine the structure of one's internal experience, by direct observation of a person's behavioral manifestations of internal responses (breathing, posture, voice tone, eye movements, etc.), and by well-formed questions.

Embedded Command Nesting a command in a sentence so that it is grammatically not a command : e.g. "It might be worthwhile considering how to do that!"

Enneagram of Character Fixation A system for describing the structure of ego.

Eye Accessing Cues Movements of a person's eyes that indicate the representation system being used.

Firing an Anchor Repeating the overt behavior - touch, gesture, voice tone, etc. - that triggers a certain response.

Flexibility Having more than one behavioral choice in a situation.

Future Pace Rehearsing in all systems so that a specific behavior or set of behaviors become linked and sequenced in response to the appropriate cues, so that it will occur naturally and automatically in future situations.

Gustatory The sense of taste.

Incongruent When two or more of a person's representations, parts, or programs are in conflict.

Integrating Responses Eliciting responses simultaneously in order to promote integration of the experience.

Internal Representation The configuration of information you create and store in your mind in the form of pictures, sounds, smells, feelings and tastes.

Kinesthetic The sense of feeling. (sensations, emotions)

Lead System The representation system initially used to access stored information.

Leading Guiding another person in a specific direction.

Leela The Divine Play of the Self.

Map of Reality A person's perceptions of events.

Maya Illusory world.

Meaning Reframing Ascribing a new meaning to a behavior/response without changing the context, usually by directing attention to deleted aspects.

Meta-model A set of language patterns that focuses attention on how people delete, distort, generalize, limit or specify their realities. It provides a series of outcome specification questions useful for recovering lost or unspecified information, and for loosening rigid patterns of thinking.

Meta-outcome The outcome of the outcome: one that is more general and basic than the stated one; "If you had that, what will that get you?"

Metaphor A story, parable or analogy that relates one's situation, experience or phenomenon to another.

Milton-model A set of language patterns useful for delivering a message in such a way that the person readily accepts it and responds to it.

Mirroring Matching one's behavior to that of another person, usually to establish rapport. Preparatory to leading or intervening.

Modality One of the five senses.

Model A description of how something works. When we say "someone's model of the world" we mean the composite of his beliefs, internal process, and behavior that allows his model to work in a certain way. A model is a way of organizing experience.

Modeling Observing and specifying how something happens, or how someone thinks or behaves, and then demonstrating the process for others so that they can learn to do it.

Negative Command An embedded command that is grammatically stated in the negative; e.g. "Wouldn't that be a great idea!"

Nest To fit one thing (outcome, story, etc.) within another.

Observer A dissociated position from which you can observe or review events, seeing yourself and others interact.

Olfactory The sense of smell.

Outcome Desired goal or result.

Pacing Matching and mirroring another person's verbal/non verbal behavior. Done subtly, it helps create a feeling of rapport between two people.

Preparatory to leading or intervening. This may mean adopting parts of another person's behavior - such as a particular gesture, facial expression, forms of speech, tone of voice, and so on.

Parts A metaphoric term for different facets of a person's behaviors, strategies, programs and personality. Parts are distinct from the specific behaviors adopted by the "parts" in order to get their positive outcome.

Perceptual Filters An attitude, point of view, perspective or set of assumptions or presuppositions about the object, person or situation.

Polarity Response A response which reverses, negates or takes the opposite position of a previous statement.

Predicates Process words: Words that express action or relationship with respect to a subject (verbs, adverbs and adjectives).

Preferred Representational System The representational system which a person habitually uses to process information or experiences: usually the one with which the person can make the most detailed distinctions.

Quotes A method used to express a message as if someone else said it; e.g. "and then he said to the audience, 'what if you could listen to silence.'"

Rapport A condition in which responsiveness has been established, often described as feeling safe or trusting, or willing.

Reframing A process by which a person's perception of a specific event or behavior is altered, resulting in a different response. Usually subdivided into Context Reframing, Meaning Reframing, and Six Step Reframing.

Representation The internal representations of experience in the five senses: seeing (visual), hearing (auditory), feeling (kinesthetic), tasting (gustatory), and smelling (olfactory).

Representational System One of the five primary senses.

Resource State The experience of useful response: an ability, attitude, behavior, characteristic, perspective or quality that is useful in some context.

Samadhi Absorption in Bliss.

Samskaras Past tendencies; impressions created by previous desires, thoughts and actions.

Satsang Association with the Truth.

Sattvic Pure/clear.

Secondary Gain The positive intention or desired outcome (often obscure or unknown) of an undesired behavior.

Sensory Acuity The process of our ability to make distinctions among the visual, auditory, kinesthetic, olfactory and gustatory systems. This gives us fuller, richer sensory experiences and the ability to create detailed sensory-based descriptions from our interaction with the external world.

Sensory-based Using words that convey information that is directly observable, verifiable by your five senses. An experience that is processed on the level of what can be seen, heard, felt, smelt and/or tasted.

Shakti Divine energy.

Six-Step Reframing A step by step process in which undesirable behavior is metaphorically separated from the desired outcome of the "part" generating the behavior, so that the part can more easily adopt new behaviors that satisfy its positive intention and that do not have the undesirable side effects of the original behavior.

Sorting Polarities Separating tendencies or "parts" that pull a person in opposite directions, into clearly defined and organized entities, preparatory to integration at the level of outcomes.

State A state of being, or a condition of body/mind response or experience at a particular moment.

Stealing an Anchor Identifying a mutually-occuring anchored sequence (stimulus-response) and then firing that anchor rather than establishing an arbitrary anchor for the response.

Stimulus-Response The repeated association between an experience and a particular response (Pavlovian conditioning) such that the stimulus becomes a trigger or cue for the response.

Submodalities The sub classifications of external experience: a picture has brightness, distance and depth. Sounds have volume, location, tone, etc.

Vasanas Latent tendencies, repressed subconscious identification.

Visual The sense of seeing.

Well-formed Outcomes A Desired State that is appropriately specified, obtainable, chunked-down and contextualized, and either helps satisfy, or does not interfere with other outcomes one may have.

The Leela School of Awakening

Client Practice Session Feedback Form

To be filled out by the Client

Name of True Friend: Date of session:

What kind of questions did the practitioner ask at the beginning of the session, and was it helpful?

Did the practitioner guide you into a relaxed state?

If yes, how was it? Describe your experience of being guided into a relaxed state.

Did the practitioner guide you to discover something in a relaxed state?

If yes, how did they do this? Please describe in brief:

How was your experience?

What did you learn from the session?

What was the best part of the session?

Any part of the session that didn't work?

Was the practitioner in rapport with you throughout the session? In other words, did you feel connected to the practitioner the entire time?

Did they say or do anything that felt out of rapport or that was out of connection with you?

Did the practitioner establish and clarify a condition that you had and help you discover what you really wanted?

Would you recommend this person to someone you know?

Would you recommend this person to someone you know for a paid session?

Why?

Anything else?

I have read and understand the information provided regarding the core goals and values of the Leela School. I willingly give my consent that the processes, material and insights revealed in this session will be used for discussion, training and teaching purposes between my True Friend and their Leela School mentor(s) and teachers.

Name (print): _____

Signature: _____

Date: _____

The Leela School of Awakening

TRUE FRIEND PRACTICE SESSION FEEDBACK FORM

To be filled out by the True Friend

Name of True Friend: Name of Client:

Date:

Present Condition:

Desired Condition:

What trance induction did you use?

Did they go into trance? How do you know?

On a scale of 1 to 5, how would you rate your ability to do the trance induction):

What therapeutic intervention did you use?

Was the intervention appropriate and effective?   How do you know?

Did the client have an insight?   How do you know?

On a scale of 1 to 5, how would you rate your ability and confidence to do the intervention:

Were you in rapport throughout the session?   How do you know?

Were you able to be a True Friend throughout the session?   How do you know?

What did you learn about being a True Friend:

Give a brief summary of your session with this person. How was it successful? Where is improvement needed?

Notes:

PERFORMANCE ASSESSMENT RUBRIC

Performance Standards	Criteria				Points
	1	2	3	4	
Demonstrates ability as a True Friend: to have a silent mind and an open heart, and not take anything personally.	You and your personality veil the interaction with the client	You attempt to discover what the client wants, and attempt to meet the client's needs	You demonstrate the capacity to discover what the client wants, and meet the client's needs, at whatever level of intervention is required. You demonstrate capacity to recognize feedback and adapt in session; you demonstrate ability to have the client realize what is needed instead of telling the client in session	You exhibit the three principles of a True Friend: (a) There is no failure, only feedback; (b) Everyone has all the resources they need already; and (c) You can only guide someone to the depth of realization that you have gone yourself.	——
Capacity to stay in rapport and discover what is wanted -	You demonstrate few elements of rapport with client in session; You demonstrate inadequate pacing and leading in session	You demonstrate less than 3 elements of rapport with client in session; You demonstrate inconsistent pacing and leading in session	You demonstrate at least 3 elements of rapport with client in session; You demonstrate effective pacing and leading in session	You demonstrate many elements of rapport with client in session; You demonstrate highly effective pacing and leading in session	——

Performance Standards	Criteria				Points
	1	2	3	4	
Demonstrates ability to elicit present and desired condition.	You ask about the present and desired condition without establishing underlying conditions	You touch briefly and superficially on underlying structure of present condition and desired condition	You delineate in more detail the structure of the present and desired condition allowing for the client to discover something as well as giving a foundation for the trance induction and intervention	You elicit in great detail and using intuitive questioning the superficial and underlying present condition and desired condition.	

Performance Standards	Criteria				Points
	1	2	3	4	
Successfully induce a trance in multiple different ways	You successfully induce a trance in less than two different ways	You successfully induce a trance two different ways	You successfully induce a trance three different ways	You successfully induce a trance in manifold different ways	_____
Perform and demonstrate multiple successful, varied therapeutic interventions	You demonstrate less than two successful, varied therapeutic interventions	You demonstrate two successful, varied therapeutic interventions	You demonstrate three successful, varied therapeutic interventions	You perform and demonstrate multiple successful, varied therapeutic interventions	_____
Evaluate the outcomes and effectiveness of treatment to inform future plans and actions	You do not recognize the importance of building review, reflection and evaluation into treatment planning.	You vaguely recognize the importance of building review, reflection and evaluation into treatment planning.	You exhibit recognition of the importance of building review, reflection and evaluation into treatment planning.	You exhibit recognition of the importance of building review, reflection and evaluation into treatment planning; and, you exhibit recognition of the importance of taking a critical approach in relation to methodologies selection	_____

Criteria Key: 4 = highly effective, 3 = effective, 2 = improvement necessary, 1 = does not meet standard

Evaluator Name: _____

Evaluator Signature: _____

Student Name: _____

Student Signature: _____

Date: _____

Comments: _____

_____

Eli Jaxon-Bear started training therapists at Esalen Institute in 1983. He integrated Ericksonian and Clinical Hypnosis with his unique view of the psyche in developing a new method of psychotherapy.

At the First International Enneagram Conference at Stanford University in 1992, Eli Jaxon-Bear presented a radically new model of the structure of the soul and psyche based on The Enneagram of Liberation. By joining self-inquiry with his map of ego fixation, he has presented a model for universal self-realization.

He founded the *Leela Foundation* in 1995, and in 2005 he founded the *Leela School of Awakening* operating in Sydney, Australia, Amsterdam, the Netherlands and Ashland, Oregon in the US.

He has been living with his partner and wife since 1976. They currently reside in Ashland, Oregon.

Eli meets people and teaches through the Leela Foundation, www.leela.org, and The Leela School of Awakening, www.leelaschool.org

Made in the USA
Middletown, DE
23 October 2023

41307459R00172